BE A FISH

The swim coaching bible to teach you to swim like a pro via swimming training, swim drills, swimmers speed secret lessons, speed strokes for beginners, adults, teens, kids, girls & boys

Sam Humphries

SAM HUMPHRIES

https://know.howtobeon.top/healthy

No part of this book may be reproduced or transmitted in any form whatsoever, electronic, or mechanical, including photocopying, recording, or by any informational storage or retrieval system without express permission from the author

Copyright © 2022 Zee Publishing
All rights reserved

INTRODUCTION

Although swimming has been part of the Olympics for decades, many people still learn the basics. Various moves and styles of swimming challenge the body, so some treat it as a great and enjoyable workout and hobby. For others, swimming is a way to express themselves freely since they feel free underwater. Plus, it's a great way for them to relax and get healthy. I don't even think learning to swim is optional. This is a MANDATORY skill everyone should know about!

In this book, you'll be taken on a journey into optimizing swimming strength and conditioning. You'll learn how to be strong and be conditioned in the many areas of the swimming arts. These exercises can complement your work in the pool and enhance your performance.

In Triathlon, you will always be limited as a triathlete unless you are a skilled swimmer. You can improve your swimming ability to the point where it significantly improves your overall performance in the sport.

Americans have been at the forefront of a worldwide fitness revolution for the last two decades due to a burgeoning national interest in better health, self-improvement, personal growth, and a desire to add more momentum to their lives. However, media coverage of the fitness craze, which appears to be focused on virtually all activities except swimming, suggests otherwise. Swimming rarely penetrates the television-controlled consciousness of the American public because it does not create a lucrative market for equipment and clothing for potential sponsors. What was an advantage for the individual swimmer now becomes a disadvantage for the sport. After all, swimmers are less visible than runners.

We begin with self-reflection on why you swim and how to prioritize and create an action plan to accomplish your goals.

WHAT INSPIRES YOU?

Coaches know that swimmers who participate in regular training are more likely to continue their involvement in the sport. People motivated to swim have an easier time getting into the pool, which means they are more likely to succeed. Often, swimmers use specific, repeatable test sets to monitor their progress in the pool.

Using these test sets or benchmark sets can help individuals set goals. Many variables can be tracked, including heart rate, split times on the pace clock, stroke lengths, and work-to-rest ratio. Scientists interested in swimming are captivated by fluid dynamics and the secrets of fast swimming. Swimming is an ever-evolving sport, and swimmers never stop improving their technique.

Take a swim class or watch a video of a top swimmer, and you'll never miss an opportunity to improve your swimming technique. Many enroll in an adult swim program or a Masters's swim program. Those who want to compete as master swimmers will have many options. When planning a training program for competitive swimmers, they should consult a coach to ensure their efforts sync with their competitions. Most master swimmers who combine regular training with a healthy diet lose weight because weight loss is about burning more calories than you consume. Many master swimmers spend their time in the pool relaxing after a long day at the office or caring for their families.

They share a trait with competitive swimmers: they can put their worries aside as soon as they step into the water. Being fit and reaching your swimming goals increases your self-esteem and influences every aspect of your life, including how you relate to others and your career.

Structured swim workouts foster a unique camaraderie among the participants because they emphasize working as a team. The closest friendships are often formed while swimming for a long time. Swimming in a structured training group can bring together swimmers of all ages, abilities, and levels of commitment into a single cohesive unit as soon as practice begins. When you're in a group, you get what you want from the workout while having fun with your friends.

TO ACHIEVE THE GOAL

Putting a long-term dream and goal into an actionable timeline may seem impossible. Swimmers can more easily write their plans and concentrate on their vision if they gradually improve their skills. Many swimmers' success hinges on the technical aspects of their training, which are all too often ignored.

The basic conditioning stroke is the most popular for triathletes and many fitness swimmers. The backstroke, with a similar beat to the freestyle, follows next. Backstroke swimmers use a combination of freestyle and backstroke muscles, which creates a dynamic balance between the two strokes. Butterflies and breaststrokes share many characteristics and progressions with the backstroke.

According to most people, swimming is a necessary sport. Afterall majority of the earth is comprised of water. Everyone needs to be able to swim!

Due to its low impact on previously untrained muscles and joints, swimming is ideal for those looking to maximize their overall fitness. As a result, you can achieve and maintain a physically fit and healthy body that's resistant to disease and injury and looks great.

Diabetes, asthma, arthritis, heart disease, and other diseases can be fought better with the healthy changes your body undergoes when pursuing this sport.

NUTRITION

Enhancing the concept of maintaining a healthy diet and regular exercise, it's important to delve into the specifics of how these practices contribute to optimal energy production and muscular performance. A balanced diet rich in macronutrients—carbohydrates, proteins, and fats—provides the necessary fuel for the body's energy systems.

To optimize your athletic performance and recovery, it's crucial to have a comprehensive understanding of nutrition and its role in your training regimen. A well-crafted diet is not just about the macronutrients—carbohydrates, proteins, and fats—but also about the timing, quality, and balance of these nutrients to support your specific training needs.

Understanding Your Goals and Nutritional Needs
Setting Clear Objectives: Before you can create an effective diet plan, you need to have clear goals. Are you aiming to improve endurance, increase strength, reduce body fat, or prepare for a competition? Each goal requires a tailored approach to nutrition.

Energy Requirements: Your energy needs fluctuate based on the intensity and duration of your workouts. On days with high-intensity training or long sessions, your carbohydrate intake will need to be higher to provide adequate fuel. Conversely, on rest days or light training days, your energy requirements will be lower.

Macronutrient Breakdown
Carbohydrates: Carbohydrates are your body's primary energy source during high-intensity exercise. Quality matters—opt

for complex carbohydrates like whole grains, legumes, and vegetables, which provide sustained energy release, rather than simple sugars that can lead to energy spikes and crashes.

Proteins: Proteins are the building blocks of muscle repair and growth. Include a variety of protein sources such as lean meats, fish, dairy, eggs, and plant-based options like tofu and legumes to ensure a complete amino acid profile.

Fats: Healthy fats are essential for overall health, hormone production, and as an energy source during prolonged, low-intensity exercise. Focus on unsaturated fats found in nuts, seeds, avocados, and fatty fish.

NUTRIENT TIMING

Pre-Workout: A meal or snack before exercising should be rich in carbohydrates and moderate in protein to fuel your workout. Avoid high-fat foods that can slow digestion.

Post-Workout: The "anabolic window" is the optimal period for nutrient intake to aid in recovery. Aim to consume a mix of carbohydrates and protein within 30 minutes to two hours post-exercise to replenish glycogen stores and repair muscle tissues.

Hydration
Hydration is Key: Water plays a critical role in nutrient transport and temperature regulation. Ensure you're well-hydrated before, during, and after workouts.

Weight Management
Caloric Balance: For weight loss, focus on creating a caloric deficit through a combination of diet and exercise. However, ensure that the deficit is not so significant that it impairs recovery or performance.

PRACTICAL TIPS FOR MEAL PLANNING

Variety and Flexibility: Incorporate a wide range of foods to cover all micronutrient needs. Be flexible with your diet to accommodate changes in training load and personal life.

Meal Prep: Prepare meals in advance to ensure you have the right foods available when you need them, especially after workouts when you may not feel like cooking.

Listen to Your Body: Pay attention to how different foods and timing affect your energy levels and performance. Adjust your diet accordingly.

A diet that supports your athletic goals is not just about the individual nutrients but about the holistic approach to what you eat, when you eat, and how those foods work in synergy with your training. By understanding the principles of sports nutrition and applying them to your daily routine, you can enhance your performance, speed up recovery, and achieve your fitness goals.

Remember, nutrition is highly individualized, and what works for one athlete may not work for another. It's essential to experiment and find the best approach that suits your body and your training demands. If you're unsure where to start or need more personalized advice, consider consulting with a sports nutritionist who can help you develop a plan tailored to your specific needs and goals.

THE KIND OF TRAINING

Incorporating a variety of exercises that target different energy systems is key to a well-rounded training regimen. For instance, high-intensity interval training (HIIT) can significantly enhance aerobic capacity by pushing the cardiovascular system to adapt to and recover from short bursts of intense activity. This type of training can lead to improvements in VO2 max, the maximum amount of oxygen the body can utilize during exercise, which is a critical determinant of endurance performance.

Conversely, long-duration, low-intensity exercise plays a role in active recovery, helping to clear metabolic byproducts and deliver nutrients to fatigued muscles. However, to optimize anaerobic performance, which is necessary for high-intensity, short-duration efforts like sprinting, athletes must engage in specific anaerobic training. This includes activities like sprint intervals, which improve the body's ability to generate energy without oxygen and tolerate the accumulation of lactate.

Swimming at or faster than race pace is not only about improving the physical aspects of performance but also about fine-tuning the neuromuscular pathways. This type of training enhances the swimmer's ability to execute precise movements at high speeds, which is crucial for maintaining technique under fatigue. For example, a swimmer might perform a set of 50-meter sprints focusing on maintaining a high elbow catch in freestyle, ensuring that even as the body tires, the stroke remains efficient and powerful.

When it comes to stroke-specific training, each style requires a tailored approach. For instance, breaststroke's unique undulating motion demands a focus on timing and coordination, which can be honed through drills that isolate the kick and pull. Incorporating drills that emphasize the glide phase can also help swimmers find the optimal balance between power and efficiency.

Strength training outside of the water is equally important. Dryland exercises such as squats, deadlifts, and plyometrics build the muscular strength and explosive power that swimmers can translate into faster starts, turns, and overall speed in the water. Core strength is particularly vital for maintaining body alignment and facilitating the transfer of power through the stroke.

Acclimatization to cold water is a gradual process that involves controlled and progressive exposure. This can be achieved through a structured program where the duration and frequency of cold-water immersion are slowly increased. The body adapts by improving circulation and metabolic processes, which can enhance the swimmer's ability to maintain core temperature and function in cold environments.

Finally, the discipline of personal and social self-control extends beyond the pool. Athletes should embody the values and behaviors that contribute to team cohesion and success. This might include adherence to team policies on attendance, punctuality, and academic performance, as well as demonstrating respect and support for teammates and coaches. By fostering a culture of excellence and accountability, swimmers can collectively push towards higher levels of performance.

PRE-WORKOUT NUTRITION

Carbohydrates and low-fat protein should be the bulk of your pre-workout snack. Having more time before your workout allows you to eat more food and consume more low-fat protein.

To ensure that you are properly hydrated for your workout, always have a drink with your snack. Water, juice, and sports drinks are all good options. Candy, high-protein bars, high-protein shakes, French fries, cookies, sodas, and energy drinks are inappropriate for pre-workout snacks. Many studies on athletes have shown that pre-workout snacking improves performance significantly compared to not eating.

Have a snack before heading to the pool to avoid hypoglycemia.

POST-WORKOUT NUTRITION

You need to know what you want to accomplish with your diet and how to get there. Creating a diet that meets your energy needs while also allowing you to adapt to the varying demands of your exercise regimen is an equally significant consideration when making a nutritionally sound meal plan. Although carbs are an essential fuel source, the amount consumed depends on the day's workout and, therefore, is unpredictable. Protein is critical for muscle growth and recovery, but a well-rounded diet that includes many common foods provides more than enough. Weight loss can be achieved by increasing your daily caloric intake by following sound dietary principles.

Once your workout is over, you should not disregard the importance of proper nutrition. After a workout, you need to refuel, repair, and hydrate your body.

Your muscle energy reserves are depleted at the end of a grueling workout. To replenish your muscle energy stores, you must consume carbohydrates as soon as possible. It takes 24 to 48 hours for your body to refuel muscle energy reserves fully. When it comes to your next workout, the sooner you start consuming carbohydrates, the more energy you will have. In the first 30 minutes after exercise, your body converts carbohydrates into muscle energy at the fastest rate and continues to do so for two hours.

Taking longer than two hours to eat something to refuel after a workout could result in a lack of energy for the next one.

We've all heard that protein is essential to building muscles. Carbohydrates, on the other hand, are required to speed up protein transport to the muscles. Carbohydrates are broken down into glucose, and proteins are broken down into amino acids in the digestive process.

FATS

Extremely fit athletes have a body fat percentage that is not significantly higher than the average competitive swimmer.

Despite eating a lot of fat, people in Greece and other Mediterranean countries had low rates of heart disease, according to a large study conducted in the 1960s. Olive oil, which is abundant in monounsaturated fatty acids, was their diet's primary fat source. Omega-3 fatty acids are typically deficient in most people's diets, even though they make up most omega-6 fats. Foods high in omega-3 fatty acids include fish, flaxseed meal, chia seeds, and walnuts, to name a few.

Women's breasts are made of fatty tissue, and women have more internal fat to protect their reproductive organs, so they tend to have higher body fat percentages than men. These numbers are dangerously close to the point where your health is in danger. Regardless of whether you gain or lose weight, by the time you reach your forties, you have an unhealthy amount of body fat. Heart disease, diabetes, cancer, and many other illnesses are linked to obesity.

Swimming by itself does not provide the training necessary to help swimmers reach their full potential. Make an effort to keep your workouts fresh by incorporating something different. While swimming, you should work on your fitness and body fat percentage. Swimmers must be measured to see if a dietary adjustment is necessary, although this is an inconvenient fact of the sport. Only the results of their tests should concern your swimmers. Because each test is a barometer only for the individual swimmer, it is inappropriate to draw comparisons with other swimmers. When swimmers eat foods with a lower fat content, they see a decrease in their skinfold measurements.

HYDRATION

Drinking sugary drinks, soft drinks, sodas, and caffeinated beverages in excess can dehydrate you and do not provide nutrients. Remember that you should drink sports drinks only during training or competition.

Failure to replace these fluids regularly during exercise will result in dehydration. A lack of oxygen will also harm the muscles that are being used. Drinking plenty of water before, during, and after swimming is the most effective way to avoid dehydration and keep the body's fluid balance in check. After your workout, weigh yourself to see if you have gained or lost weight.

It's important to remember to replenish your body's fluids after a workout by drinking three cups of fluid for every pound lost.

You should drink sports drinks or water from your water bottle immediately after warming up and after each race to rehydrate your body. Snacks should be kept cool and easy to eat by packing a cold pack in your bag.

TRAINING

Before we go any further, please take note of this link. It has swimming-related instructional videos, that will complement the teachings in this book.

The link is: https://know.howtoalways.win/swimming

This hard-earned aerobic potential will be put to waste if you can't swim well enough to put it to proper use. For the triathletes reading this book, swimming consumes a disproportionate amount of the energy available for the entire race, accounting for only a tiny portion of the total race distance and time. Generally, triathletes don't just care about how slowly they paddle. Rather than swimming faster, you will improve your overall performance by conserving energy for the bike and run.

Even better, you'll be able to swim faster if you improve your swimming efficiency.

A swim-specific workout considers the different races, the muscle groups used, and the training intervals and times required. Whether you want to swim your fastest 200-meter butterfly or your strongest 100-m freestyle, ask yourself whether endurance-only training is the most effective way to get there.

To get the most out of your training, ensure you have a clear idea of what you want to achieve before you begin. Once your workout's objective is clear, you can devise an effective training strategy. Interval training is a simple way to spice up your workout routine, whether you're a novice or a seasoned athlete.

Others prefer to swim at sunrise or sunset, while others do so in the daytime. Most swimmers who are initially reluctant to swim at night do so to prepare for a marathon that begins or ends at night. The phenomenon of bioluminescence only occurring at night in saltwater fascinates many swimmers, although they may never have a reason or motivation to swim initially.

TEAM DYNAMICS

Team dynamics play a pivotal role in the training environment, serving as a catalyst for peak performance among athletes. The camaraderie and collective drive within a team can significantly elevate an individual's motivation, pushing them to transcend their perceived limits. When teammates exhibit unwavering dedication and offer consistent encouragement, it fosters a competitive yet supportive atmosphere that is conducive to personal and group excellence.

The influence of team dynamics extends beyond the pool or track; it permeates into every aspect of an athlete's regimen. By setting higher standards of performance and fostering a culture of excellence, teammates challenge one another to strive for their personal best. This healthy competition is not about outdoing each other but about elevating the entire team's performance.

Moreover, the support system that teammates provide is integral to an athlete's success. They understand the rigors of training and the importance of recovery, often sharing tips and strategies for effective rest and optimal nutrition. This collective knowledge and shared experience reinforce the importance of a holistic approach to training, which includes prioritizing sleep, rest, and proper nutrition. These elements are crucial for maintaining high energy levels, ensuring quick recovery, and ultimately, achieving top performance.

In essence, the synergy of a team can be a powerful force, inspiring each member to push boundaries and achieve goals that may seem unattainable in isolation. The encouragement from peers, the shared commitment to goals, and the mutual pursuit of excellence are what make team dynamics an indispensable element of athletic training and success.

HEART RATES

You'll need to monitor your heart rate and breathing to get the most out of your workouts. Consult your doctor if you're over 35 before starting a fitness program. The same rule applies to you if you are under thirty-five years old and have significant risk factors for heart disease, such as high blood pressure. Once given the all-clear, you'll have to decide how hard you want to exercise your heart and lungs.

This is the number of heartbeats per minute, known as the heart rate. Your heart rate is the most accurate indicator. If you've never worked out before, your resting heart rate is the number.

After that, you need to figure out your maximum heart rate, which is the number of beats per minute a heart of your age should be able to produce.

Your exercise range is the range in which you want to keep your heart rate during exercise so that it is high enough to benefit your heart but not so high that it is a danger to you. This is an important number to know.

PLANNED COURSES OF STUDY

Structured training programs can significantly enhance a swimmer's technique, speed, and confidence. Transitioning from casual, unstructured swimming to a well-designed training regimen can yield noticeable improvements. It's a common misconception that master swim programs are exclusively for seasoned swimmers with a deep passion for the sport. However, these programs are inclusive and cater to a range of skill levels, from beginners to advanced competitors. In fact, many newcomers are often surprised to find peers who are also just starting their swimming journey.

Master swim programs are not one-size-fits-all; they offer a variety of workouts that allow swimmers to train at their own pace within their designated lanes. A survey by the United States Masters Swimming (USMS) revealed that less than a third of Masters swimmers identify as competitive athletes, highlighting the diversity within these programs.

When designing a swimming workout, various elements can be adjusted to meet specific goals. For instance, swimmers can focus on refining their technique rather than simply increasing resistance, akin to lifting weights. Group workouts can be compared to circuits, where a collection of exercises is performed in succession, tailored to individual strength and endurance objectives.

It's important to note that not all workouts are suitable for every swimmer. To achieve significant muscle growth, a regimen of medium-to-heavy repetitions with moderate resistance is often recommended. Contrary to the fear of becoming overly bulky, incorporating a few dryland sessions per week won't lead to excessive muscle mass. Instead, these sessions should involve fewer repetitions (about 3–6) with heavier weights or resistance to effectively enhance strength and power for swimmers.

Understanding the distinction between a structured training program and basic swimming lessons is crucial. Structured programs are designed to improve swimming efficiency through drills and tips provided by on-deck coaches, who can observe and correct technique throughout the workout, especially when fatigue sets in.

Most master swimming programs employ coaches responsible for developing training plans and offering guidance during sessions. In some rural areas, swimmers may opt to train independently or in informal groups, potentially missing out on the benefits of professional coaching, which can include stroke clinics and underwater video analysis to further refine their skills.

Coaches often group swimmers by ability to provide customized training for each lane, ensuring that everyone's needs and capabilities are addressed. For those new to swimming with a team, it's common to start with freestyle workouts and gradually learn other strokes, turns, and sequences. However, without proper coaching, joining a Masters swim team may only offer marginal improvement compared to solo training.

The commitment to attend practice is essential, as even the best master's program cannot benefit a swimmer who is not present. Masters swimming attracts individuals from various backgrounds and skill levels, offering a supportive environment for those aged 18 to 88 to reengage with the sport. Regardless of experience, it's important for newcomers to focus on stretching, technique, and to seek advice from a coach.

For those new to structured training, starting with three to four sessions per week, each lasting 20 to 30 minutes, is advisable. The initial focus should be on mastering stroke techniques and building aerobic capacity, with a coach present for safety and feedback.

As swimmers progress, they may extend their workouts and incorporate strength training circuits, which involve a series of exercises repeated multiple times. This approach effectively builds foundational strength and endurance, enhancing overall swimming performance.

TAKING A SOLO DIP IN THE POOL

Swimming techniques and workout planning are among the many topics covered by a growing number of websites aimed at helping swimmers who prefer to train alone. Individual swimmers should know the significance of varying their workouts to achieve their fitness goals. Swimming lessons with a professional coach or at a swim school are ideal for people learning independently.

Allow enough time to warm up before beginning the main sets to maximize your workout. If you're swimming alone, your workout will begin as soon as you arrive. Keep your muscles warm once you're in the water by swimming behind the other swimmers in your lane. After your workout, make sure to put your workout gear back.

If you're new to a workout, ask the coach which lane is the easiest to acclimate. Swimmers use the terms "lane base" or "speed interval" to describe how fast swimmers swim in a pool lane. Of course, these are relative terms, and the most effective way to determine which lane is right for you is to watch the swimmers around you.

When the trainer goes over the workout's various sets, pay attention. If you're a newcomer to the exercise group, you might not fully comprehend all of the instructions. While the other swimmers in your lane begin their set, take a few extra minutes to absorb the teachings.

BREATHING

It's not uncommon for people to be able to swim freestyle without stopping to catch their breath. All four competitive swims should be easy, effortless, and repeatable when breathing in and out. Before swimming underwater, we were taught to blow bubbles as part of our swimming lessons. Even though this may sound simple, it's essential to long-term swimming, not just in freestyle but in all forms of the sport.

Many swimmers believe they must adhere to the breathing patterns they practice to succeed in the competition. Triathletes and open-water swimmers can benefit from this theory because they do not have to deal with the deflation of air during turns and can become accustomed to a comfortable bilateral breathing pattern.

Maintaining a stable posture is easier when your breathing is more relaxed. Streamlining your body in the water by focusing on breathing and maintaining proper balance is possible. The ability to breathe more efficiently is a benefit of improving your balance and form, allowing you to enjoy your time in the water more. It is helpful for swimmers to understand the water to improve their swimming technique thoroughly.

To breathe correctly, many swimmers blunder by lifting their heads and looking forward instead of down. Rather than stretching ahead, swimmers bob up and down due to these faulty positions.

Swimmers of any skill level can use Butterfly drills because of the importance of relaxation, rhythm, and timing in this stroke. The crawl and the drill are often alternatives to the butterfly stroke by novice swimmers as they learn the fundamentals. The butterfly is a very effective conditioning stroke. Once you master it, you'll be better at all other strokes because you'll have learned how to control stroke rhythm and tempo with your core.

Some elite swimmers only breathe on one side, while others simultaneously alternate between breathing on both sides. The development of the front quadrant timing relies heavily on the discipline of positioning the limbs before they touch the water.

It's common for swimmers to practice freestyle with one hand or arm extended forward until the other arm has completed its stroke cycle and "caught up" with it. Using your waiting arm, move through the catching details and pull through as soon as your stroking limb meets the waiting limb. During the catch, your main goal is to get the limb in the right position before you begin to push back. Until his left arm has completed its stroke cycle and met up with the right, he holds his right arm extended above his head.

BREATHING TECHNIQUES TO HELP YOU RELAX

Breathing techniques are a cornerstone of proficient swimming across all strokes, and mastering them can significantly enhance your comfort and performance in the water. While swimming freestyle, many individuals can maintain a flawless technique until the need to breathe disrupts their rhythm. However, effective breathing should integrate seamlessly into each stroke, whether it's freestyle, backstroke, breaststroke, or butterfly, making the action feel effortless and sustainable.

From the earliest swimming lessons, we're taught the importance of exhaling underwater—often starting with blowing bubbles. This fundamental skill is crucial for long-term success in swimming. Proper breathing relaxes not only the muscles in the face, jaw, mouth, and neck but also contributes to overall relaxation and efficiency in the water.

Consider the relaxed facial muscles you experience while running or cycling; this is the level of relaxation to aim for while swimming. Tension arises when swimmers hold their breath underwater, leading to a rushed and tense inhalation when the head surfaces. To avoid this, some swimmers exhale through both the mouth and nose, while others prefer a gentle mouth-only exhale during their stroke.

Breathing should be timed with the stroke to maintain proper form. In freestyle, for example, the breath should be taken at the beginning of the catch phase, where the hands and forearms start to pull through the water. Lifting the head too high, or keeping it out of the water for too long, can cause the hips to drop and disrupt the swimmer's forward momentum. Instead, the head should return to a neutral position quickly after the breath, with the swimmer's gaze directed down towards the bottom of the pool.

In both freestyle and backstroke, excessive head lifting during breathing can cause the hips and legs to sink, creating drag. The goal is to maintain a streamlined position, where the body is long and horizontal during the glide phase of each stroke. A neutral head position helps achieve this.

Some swimmers find using a nose plug can enhance their breathing technique, allowing them to focus on exhaling through the mouth in a controlled manner. When turning the head to breathe, a crescendo of exhalation through both the nose and mouth is common, followed by an inhalation through the mouth. This technique has been honed by swimmers over many years and includes positioning the tongue to prevent water from entering the trachea.

Even experienced swimmers may occasionally inhale water, but the key is to maintain a consistent breathing pattern. In freestyle, breaststroke, and butterfly, the exhalation typically occurs at the end of the underwater pull phase. As the body moves forward, the swimmer turns to the breathing side and lifts the face out of the water to inhale.

The timing of the breath is synchronized with the stroke: the arms pull, the hips tilt, and the head and shoulders rise out of the water to exhale. In butterfly, the exhalation happens as the body presses down and the chest rises, coinciding with the face emerging from the water. Backstroke, while different in that the face remains out of the water, still requires a rhythmic pattern of inhalation and exhalation to maintain efficiency.

By focusing on these breathing techniques and incorporating them into your training, you can improve your relaxation in the water, reduce drag, and maintain a consistent and powerful stroke across all swimming disciplines.

SWIMMING AND BREATHING WITH A FLUTTER SET

Enhancing your swimming performance and breath control through land-based exercises can be highly effective. To optimize the benefits of a flutter kick set while seated, consider the following enhanced routine:

First, select a sturdy chair and position yourself at the edge with your legs extended straight in front of you. Engage your core muscles to support your posture, ensuring that your back is straight and not slouched. This alignment is crucial as it mimics the streamlined position you aim for in the water.

Initiate the flutter kick motion with pointed toes, a technique swimmers use to maximize propulsion in the water. The movement should originate from your hips, with minimal bending at the knees, to accurately simulate the mechanics of an actual flutter kick. Maintain a consistent rhythm as you alternate kicking with each leg, focusing on quick, controlled movements.

As you perform the flutter kicks, incorporate breathing exercises to enhance your lung capacity and breath control. Practice inhaling deeply through your nose and exhaling through your mouth in a controlled manner, coordinating your breaths with the kicking rhythm. For example, you might inhale over the course of three kicks and exhale over the next three.

To further challenge your respiratory system and prepare for the demands of swimming, you can add resistance to your breaths. This can be done by pursing your lips during exhalation, which creates a slight back pressure and simulates the resistance experienced when exhaling underwater.

In addition to strengthening your legs and abdomen, this exercise also serves as a valuable opportunity to practice maintaining a relaxed facial expression and jaw while breathing, as tension in these areas can hinder efficient breathing during swimming.

By dedicating time to this enhanced flutter kick and breathing set on land, you will build the muscular endurance and breath control needed for effective swimming. This preparation will facilitate a smoother transition to the pool, where you can apply these refined techniques to your swimming strokes, ultimately leading to improved performance and stamina in the water.

FLUTTER STEP IN THE PRONE POSITION WITH CONTROLLED BREATHING

The flutter kick in the prone position, paired with controlled breathing, is a fundamental skill that enhances your swimming efficiency and helps build endurance. As you hold onto the pool's edge, ensure your body is aligned in a streamlined position, with your face down in the water, looking directly at the bottom of the pool.

Begin the flutter kick by engaging your core and hip flexors, keeping your legs straight and your toes pointed. The motion should be generated from the hips, with minimal bend in the knees, creating a small, rapid, and consistent kick. Your ankles should be flexible, acting like flippers to provide propulsion.

As you execute the flutter kick, focus on your breathing technique. Inhale quickly and deeply through your mouth when you turn your head to the side, ensuring that your mouth clears the water's surface. It's important to keep your movements fluid and avoid lifting your head too high, as this can disrupt your body's horizontal alignment.

Exhale steadily and completely underwater, either through your nose, mouth, or both, depending on your comfort level. This exhalation should be controlled and prolonged, allowing you to maintain a relaxed state and prepare for the next inhalation.

Integrating the flutter kick with controlled breathing requires synchronization. Establish a rhythm where your breaths are timed with your kicks. For instance, you might take a breath every three or four kicks, depending on your lung capacity and comfort level.

As you become more proficient with this exercise, you can gradually move away from the pool's edge and practice maintaining your balance and coordination in open water. This will help you develop the skills necessary for continuous swimming without the support of the poolside.

Remember to maintain a relaxed facial expression and avoid tensing up, as this can hinder your breathing and overall performance. With practice, the combination of flutter kicking and controlled breathing will become second nature, contributing to a more efficient and effective swimming technique.

A FLUTTER KICK, FOLLOWED BY A STEADY INHALATION

To refine your flutter kick and breathing synchronization, it's essential to focus on maintaining proper body alignment and integrating the arm movements with rhythmic breathing. Begin by ensuring your head and pelvis are aligned correctly, with your gaze directed straight down at the pool floor. This position helps maintain a streamlined form, reducing drag and allowing for more efficient movement through the water.

If you notice any sagging in your body position, it's a sign to check your arm extension. Your arms should be straight, providing the necessary support and alignment for your body. This also sets the stage for a powerful arm pull, which is integral to propulsion in strokes like freestyle and backstroke.

As you work on refining your technique, focus on incremental improvements. Start by mastering the arm movement, ensuring that each stroke is deliberate and controlled. Then, incorporate rhythmic breathing, which involves timing your breaths with the strokes. For instance, in freestyle, you might breathe every three strokes, which helps maintain a balanced rotation and ensures that you're not favoring one side over the other.

To practice on land, simulate the swimming motion by standing in chest-high water and leaning forward until the water reaches your shoulders. Extend your left arm straight in front of you, keeping it steady, and allow your right arm to drop into the water. Rest your left cheek on your left arm while turning your head to the right to breathe. This drill helps you get accustomed to the feeling of alternating arm movements with breathing to the side.

The catch-up drill, where one arm waits for the other to catch up before starting its stroke, can be particularly useful for developing a smooth and synchronized stroke. This drill encourages a pause that gives you time to focus on your breathing pattern, ensuring that you're not rushing your breaths or your arm movements.

By practicing these techniques consistently, you'll develop muscle memory and the coordination needed to combine a steady flutter kick with controlled inhalation and arm movements. The goal is for these actions to become second nature, allowing you to swim with greater efficiency and speed.

THE FIRST STEP TO BECOMING A FISH IS TO LEARN HOW TO BALANCE

As children, we all learned to move, balance, lift, climb and carry ourselves without being guided to do so. Adults rarely have the opportunity to learn naturally in the water because we're not familiar with it and because swimming lessons are usually taught that way. When we teach swimmers to swim freestyle, we find that they worry that they aren't doing enough to maintain their fitness after doing drills for a few days. Your swimming skills will improve if you get involved in swimming with a sense of adventure and discovery, rather than focusing on efficiency or performance.

A better swimmer may swim longer and practice more often, but every stroke and lap they complete will be more productive.

Once you master balance, you can swim any distance with ease and efficiency. This is essential for mastering other swimming techniques and eventually participating in a triathlon. It's not enough to just sit back and let the water do the work for you; you've to build on it. The signs of progress happen in small steps, starting with simple movements and positions that are ideal for beginners.

The core muscles of the body are involved in the concepts of

balance and flow

Through the internal connections of the body's core, you can learn how to achieve horizontal balance while swimming by applying strong pressure to the upper chest. Swimmers with poor balance tend to move so that their hips and legs dangle below the water's surface. On the other hand, balance exercises may seem unnecessary if you are already a skilled swimmer. This is because you have completed strenuous workouts or finished the swim leg of several races in a relatively good position.

If you swim fast, you tend to lose length at the beginning of each stroke. Thanks to the progression of balance exercises, you can keep your lower body in a horizontal position in the water without pushing. The energy you expend pushing off as you swim in proper balance on the surface will propel you forward. Continue by gently pressing your chin, chin, and chest to the bottom of the pool while keeping your eyes on the ground.

With this exercise, you will not reach a horizontal position, but you will come close. When you reach the most comfortable position, slowly raise your arms above your head. Since your lungs are now closer to the center of the seesaw and your arms are extended, your lower body will rotate even higher in this position. Hold this position, especially during freestyle and backstroke.

Your goal is to achieve proper head-neck-spine alignment and a tight core by forming a long, streamlined boat. Breathing is the most common cause of a person's bad balance and posture.

Some swimmers start with a balanced freestyle body position, but then unbalance the body line by lifting their head out of the water with each breath. To avoid having to lift their head on an inhale, freestyle swimmers who learn to coordinate their breathing with the rotation of their hips and shoulders benefit greatly.

Maintaining fluidity of movement is as important as perfecting the mechanics of your drills and skills as you progress from basic balance to dynamic balance and beyond. You will learn to draw strength effortlessly when your rhythms and movements originate in your core rather than your arms and legs. Using these rhythms, you can develop a strong, efficient swimming style. The faster you swim, the more critical it is to reduce drag, as it increases exponentially with speed.

One of the defining characteristics of elite swimmers is their mastery of streamlining. These swimmers have honed the art of gliding effortlessly through the water, shaping their bodies to reduce drag with each swimming cycle.

When you are balanced, you do not waste energy against the sensation of sinking. Because of the common assumption that swimming upright is the correct posture, much energy is wasted.

More than 90% of the energy expended by novice swimmers is spent trying to avoid suffocation.

The most critical aspect of efficient freestyle swimming is a well-controlled breathing pattern. To effectively ventilate the lungs while swimming, one must master the art of breath control. Balance, relaxation, arm timing, streamlining, stroke length, and usable power are all improved by swimmers who extend their exhalation into the swim current. Swimmers who have excellent breath control exhale long after short, easy breaths.

A swimmer's ability to turn freely is compromised if they lack dynamic balance. Hours of lat pulls and tricep presses are common among these swimmers who know something is hindering them. In particular, the unbalanced swimmer tends to have a frantic movement pattern in the freestyle. Shorter and more strokes are required to maintain speed as he speeds up.

When you are not in the water, your head should remain neutral. Allow the water to take the weight off your head and find its most natural position. Stability, flexibility, and strength are the main goals of swimming-specific movements. You can improve your swimming posture and shoulder strength by working on your balance, core strength, and overall stability.

STREAMLINE

Streamlining in swimming is the art of creating a body position that minimizes resistance and maximizes propulsion, effectively connecting the upper and lower halves of the body into one cohesive unit. A stable core is essential as it serves as the foundation from which the limbs can generate and transfer force. This concept is akin to the ground effect in physics, where the force exerted by the feet against the ground is transmitted through a solid core, allowing for powerful movements.

The shape of a swimmer's body in the water has a profound impact on the level of friction encountered. Rather than maintaining a position that is perpendicular to the direction of movement, which would increase drag, proficient swimmers intuitively understand the importance of a slight tilt or rotation. This lateral inclination, which occurs during the freestyle stroke, aligns the body more closely with the flow of water, thereby reducing resistance.

To achieve a streamlined form, swimmers must focus on extending their bodies from fingertips to toes, creating a long, narrow silhouette that slices through the water. The arms should be stretched forward, biceps pressed against the ears, with hands overlapping or one on top of the other, depending on the swimmer's preference. The legs should be straight, with pointed toes, contributing to the sleek profile.

Maintaining a balanced body position throughout the stroke cycle is crucial for minimizing drag. This balance is not static but dynamic, adjusting with each stroke to maintain a streamlined trajectory. Swimmers should aim to keep their pulls long, ensuring that each arm stroke maximizes its propulsive potential without disrupting the body's streamlined position.

Streamlined exercises, often referred to as "flow shapers," are designed to heighten a swimmer's awareness of their body's interaction with the water. These drills encourage swimmers to pay close attention to how their movements affect the water pressure around them, teaching them to move with greater efficiency and less resistance. By practicing these exercises, swimmers can develop a keen sense of how to adjust their body position for optimal streamlining, leading to faster and more energy-efficient swimming.

Swimmers refine their technique and enhance their feel for the water by engaging in flow shaper exercises, which are designed to cultivate an awareness of the water's resistance and flow patterns around their bodies. A critical aspect of swimming efficiency is maintaining a consistent body position, particularly in breaststroke, where each cycle of the stroke starts and concludes in a streamlined posture.

In strokes such as backstroke, butterfly, and freestyle, a swimmer's arms and upper body may momentarily rise above the water as they recover between strokes. This action should be fluid and controlled to minimize drag and maintain forward momentum.

As swimmers pick up speed, they encounter increased frictional resistance, which can double with each increment in velocity. Therefore, adopting a long, streamlined, arrow-like body shape is essential to combat this resistance. The impact of shape drag is even more pronounced, potentially quadrupling when a swimmer doubles their speed, emphasizing the importance of maintaining an efficient form.

Executing a powerful push off the wall is the first step in leveraging this streamlined form. Swimmers should extend their arms and point their fingertips, engaging the muscles in the torso to create a rigid, hydrodynamic profile. This position is akin to a ship cutting through water, transitioning from the calm flow to the more turbulent wake of a destroyer. Initiating the movement with a head-first kick and maintaining a light, relaxed flutter kick with arms at the sides helps the swimmer glide smoothly on the water's surface.

To maximize propulsion underwater, swimmers often aim to increase their body surface area. This strategy involves ensuring that the body's frame is as hydrodynamic as possible while applying greater pressure in both the upward and downward phases of the stroke, such as in the underwater dolphin kick. The effectiveness of this technique is influenced by each swimmer's unique combination of agility, physique, and strength, which determines the power of their kicks.

It's important to note that the outer extremities of the kick will inherently have less force. To enhance kick speed, swimmers focus on increasing the distance covered per kick without sacrificing the tempo. The larger the effective body surface area, the more potential there is for forward movement. Observing elite swimmers can provide insights into the execution of an efficient underwater dolphin kick.

For a balanced and streamlined posture, swimmers can practice kicking with one arm extended forward and the other arm relaxed at their side. This drill encourages a stable core and proper alignment, simulating the sensation of falling through the water with minimal resistance. By maintaining a slight flutter kick, the swimmer can focus on the precision of their movements and the subtleties of their body position, all of which contribute to a more efficient and faster swim.

UNDERWATER RECOVERY KICK

The underwater recovery kick is a nuanced technique that can significantly enhance a swimmer's efficiency and speed. To execute this movement effectively, begin by lightly stepping forward six to ten times while extending your right arm forward, keeping your left arm relaxed at your side. As you bring your right arm forward underwater, simultaneously roll the left side of your body downward. This rolling motion is crucial as it helps to maintain a streamlined position and reduces drag. Continue the exercise by pulling the underwater arm through the water and switching to the other side, ensuring a continuous, fluid motion.

For many master swimmers, mastering the underwater recovery kick can be a challenging endeavor. It requires coordination, balance, and a strong sense of body position in the water. However, with consistent practice, swimmers can develop the skill to perform this technique with grace and efficiency.

When incorporating fins into this or any other drill, it is important for swimmers with limited ankle flexibility to exercise caution. Kicking too forcefully or relying on fins to maintain body position can lead to inefficient swimming patterns. Vertical or lateral movements that create large waves are indicative of excessive energy expenditure and increased resistance. In fact, wave resistance can double when a swimmer doubles their speed, making it essential to minimize such movements.

The forward extension of the arm and shoulder in freestyle is more than just a reach; it is an opportunity to bring the body into a more hydrodynamic position. Achieving a reduced shape and wave resistance is contingent upon regaining mobility in the shoulder and arm. Many adult swimmers have encountered obstacles due to a lack of flexibility or past injuries. It is important for each swimmer to find a position that is both comfortable and effective for their unique body mechanics and to consistently practice in that position.

Developing a keen sense of touch in the water is fundamental to a swimmer's progress. A positive water feel leads to more fluid strokes and a harmonious relationship with the water. By maintaining a long, loose, and rhythmic body line, swimmers can enhance their stroke progression. For beginners, learning to breathe comfortably and alternate breathing sides with each arm stroke is essential. Experienced swimmers often prefer to breathe every two strokes, as it provides ample oxygen for sustained effort and higher speeds. However, adopting a breathing pattern of every four, five, or six strokes can encourage swimmers to focus on refining their stroke technique.

Novice swimmers often struggle with maintaining a long body line, as their hips and legs tend to drop, and their arms do not fully extend at the front of the stroke. This truncation of the stroke can disrupt the fluidity and relaxation necessary for efficient swimming. If a swimmer has difficulty lifting their face out of the water to breathe, they should exaggerate their turn toward the breathing side to facilitate easier inhalation. This adjustment is particularly beneficial for swimmers with limited mobility in their shoulder girdle and neck or those who experience rotator cuff impingement.

As swimmers advance in skill and increase their range of motion, they can reduce their rotation and achieve a more streamlined position. This progression leads to a more efficient stroke and can significantly improve overall swimming performance.

STRENGTHENING PHASE

The core muscles, defined in this book as the area from the neck to the knees, include:

• The upper back and shoulder muscles.

• The abdominal muscles.

• The trunk and thigh muscles.

Strength in swimming comes from these muscles. The proper way to utilize this strength is to begin the freestyle underwater move known as the snatch with a strong buildup. An extremely vital part of any swimming stroke is when the swimmer's hand contacts the water, and the swimmer starts pulling. This term first became popular with freestyle and crawl swimming growth in the nineteenth century. While keeping your elbow up, you begin to pull by pushing down on your fingertips and keeping your body straight.

Imagine that your elbow is pressed against the side of the pool. Maintain the raised elbow position throughout the pull cycle once you've assumed it during the underwater pull. Use your core muscles to rotate your body beyond the catch point while keeping your hands and elbows in the water. At the midpoint of the pull, the elbow flexion is about 90 degrees, and it opens up again when the hand completes the pull.

The slow-moving hand is seen before picking up speed and moving under the hip at the end. The power phase of freestyle swimming is the acceleration of the hand through the underwater pull, synchronized with the rotation of the center of the body. After a few meters, they leave the water. The flexibility of the swimmers' shoulders and backs enables them to get into the catch position earlier in the swim stroke.

Learn the mechanics of the catch position and proper muscle tension for an efficient underwater stroke. This is done by using the following teaching sequence both on the deck and in the water. The first step is to stand erect on the pool deck. Simulate the freestyle pull by having a partner apply light pressure to your palm. Lift your elbow and squeeze your fingers together.

Use your muscles as you pull, ranging from raising your elbow, extending your arm, and lowering your elbow. Your core muscles should be engaged when you pull with your elbow raised, including your upper back, chest, and shoulders. The starting position should be full arm extension, shoulder-width apart, and slightly flexed wrists. Standing at the deepest part of your pelvis, face the wall.

Raise your body as high as you can while maintaining a high elbow position. If you're anchoring in the catch position or finishing the propulsion phase, you'll be able to easily adjust the angle of your hand to better hold the water. Smaller paddles, preferably with holes, should be used by novice swimmers at the masters' level.

TREATMENT OF THE WATER

The concept of "treatment of the water" in swimming is a fundamental aspect of stroke efficiency and effectiveness. The traditional focus for many swimmers has been on the idea of using their hands to push water towards their feet. This approach emphasizes the importance of the hand's role in propulsion, but it is a simplistic view that does not fully capture the complexity of effective swimming technique.

Swimming technique is indeed the result of countless repetitions that create deeply ingrained patterns within the nervous system, often referred to as muscle memory. These patterns are resistant to change, which is why swimmers may find it challenging to alter their stroke after years of practice. However, this resistance can be overcome with focused and deliberate practice of new techniques. For example, when considering the efficiency of a swimmer's stroke, it's not just about how much water is pushed back with each hand movement. It's also about how well the swimmer holds the water, or 'catches' it, and how effectively they use their entire body to create propulsion. This includes the rotation of the hips, the positioning of the head, and the timing of the breath.

The mention of a 25% gain in efficiency likely refers to a reduction in the number of strokes taken to cover a given distance, which is a common way to measure improvement in swimming efficiency. A lower stroke count generally indicates that a swimmer is traveling further with each stroke, which is a desirable outcome.

It's important to note that stroke rates will vary among swimmers due to differences in body size, strength, and technique. There is no universal "magic number" of strokes per lap that applies to all swimmers. Instead, each swimmer should work with their coach to determine their optimal stroke count and rate for their individual goals and abilities.

Monitoring stroke count can be a valuable tool for tracking progress and identifying areas for improvement. By counting strokes per lap during training and competition, swimmers can gain insights into their efficiency and technique. An increase in stroke count may indicate fatigue, a breakdown in technique, or a need for further skill development.

To effectively track progress, swimmers can have a teammate or coach record their stroke count for each lap and compare it to their split times. This data can help identify patterns, such as whether the stroke count increases as the swimmer becomes tired, which can inform adjustments to training and technique.

In summary, the treatment of the water in swimming is a complex interplay of various body movements and positions. Swimmers should focus on developing a holistic approach to their stroke that includes a strong catch, effective body rotation, and proper timing. By tracking stroke count and making informed adjustments, swimmers can continue to refine their technique and improve their efficiency in the water.

BACKSTROKE

The body's long axis must be rotated for each stroke, so various exercises have been chosen for freestyle and backstroke. Freestyle and backstroke swimmers must meet the following requirements. Many of the exercises can be done in either style.

Long-axis swimming refers to the fact that swimmers rotate primarily around the body's vertical axis in these two styles of swimming. A number of the greatest freestyle swimmers were also world-class backstrokers in the past. All swimming styles eventually come together when discussing stroke tempos, rhythm, and relaxation. In addition to freestyle, the backstroke is essential to any swimmer's repertoire.

It opens and strengthens the pectoral muscles, other muscle groups, and the legs. A faster freestyle and a better backstroke are expected outcomes for swimmers who devote time and effort to mastering the backstroke.

As with freestyle, the backstroke involves swimming with your arms extended out in front of you. Swimming freestyle, breaststroke, or butterfly is better for your shoulders because it provides a similar rotation but in the opposite direction. We begin by looking at the position of the head in all competitive swims.

We know that we must reduce resistance and increase propulsion to swim faster. The ideal head position for the backstroke is neutral and parallel to the spine. The most common mistake swimmers make is looking down at their feet instead of forward. Compared to freestyle, this shift in body position is even more dramatic.

Arm pulls can be started once you've found your balance in the backstroke

The idea of swimming with a cup of water on your head is less about theatrics and more about maintaining a straight head posture while in the water. By swimming with proper head posture, we want to keep our body line as neutral as possible in the water. While some swimmers can hold the shell atop their heads, they still have improper head posture. Even if you keep your forehead level, your overall head position is too high out of the water.

You lose the most water by keeping your head in line with the rest of your body and spine. In addition, your kick's amplitude should be less than half a meter in freestyle. Flutter kicks aren't as relevant as freestyle. Compared to the backstroke, freestyle lets you pull a little more water per pull and achieve an early vertical forearm with enhanced leverage.

Since swimming backstroke requires torso balance, nearly everyone who does so is familiar with it. In the backstroke, you can quickly learn to improve your balance to reduce the energy you need to put into the crawl. It is generally recommended that swimmers pull their chins into their necks and look slightly toward their feet. This is highly inconvenient, resulting in neck and back pain and a dramatic drop in your hips. Because they are afraid of getting water in their mouths or noses, inexperienced swimmers often tilt their heads backward as though they were craning their necks. This is to avoid getting water in their mouths.

As a result of this posture, the head spins away from the spine, and the hips fall forward. A swimmer's ability to turn completely and effortlessly in either direction is affected by both factors. Draw a circle 1-inch above the eyebrows, the top corner of the eye, and on the cheek under the jaw. Run under the chin and up the other side. This will help you understand proper head positioning. To kick, drill, or backstroke, only the area inside this circle should be visible above water.

This technique will provide a neutral and natural position for your head. You should keep your head stable so the glass doesn't fall over. If you want to feel how stable your head should be while swimming backstroke, you can put a half-empty water bottle on your forehead and swim a length. They do a good job keeping their heads steady with practice.

Press your "buoy" with your upper back during the backstroke. The more you use this band while swimming, the more buoyant and higher your hips will be in the water. This will reduce the amount of effort you put into the movement. You can use this technique more quickly if you are familiar with this sensation.

Several advantages can be attributed to the rocking motion

It allows you to inhale and exhale without moving your head. During the glide phase of each stroke, your body should be as streamlined, long, and horizontal as possible. Maintain a level head. A neutral head position is essential for maintaining balance in both long axes.

At the beginning of the backstroke stroke

This means that those swimmers who spend the time and effort to perfect their backstroke start will have a significant advantage over those who take their start in water for granted. Swimmers of all levels should use the steps in the following backstroke start procedure. Positioned for action. Place your feet shoulder-width apart against the pool wall, just below the water's surface, and hold on to the pool's edge or the gutter with both hands.

Even though most swimmers prefer to stagger their feet, you should choose the most comfortable position. Put your legs and arms outstretched before you, then shoot up and over the water. Repeat exercise 2 by entering the water and performing an upward kick with both feet. Take a second look at the previous exercise, but this time add some arm movement to the take-off.

Throw your arms to the side or overhead as you propel yourself forward with your legs and raise your hips above the water. Keep your body in a smooth line as you follow your fingertips through the hole with your entire frame. Maintain your streamlined shape once you've entered the water. A dolphin or flutter kick can help you regain your footing if you begin to lose momentum.

High-amplitude dolphin kicks are sometimes called the "double leg kick" because they are distinct from the dolphin kick used in butterfly swimming. You should never forget to blow your nose while submerged to keep it water-free. US Swimming and USMS stipulate that you must have your feet wholly submerged. Your knees should be bent at a 90-degree angle when you hear the command, and you should make your mark on the block.

Your legs should propel you through the water at the start of the race as you elongate your body and throw your arms back in a streamline. Practice and experiment with foot and hand positions to discover what works best for you in the backstroke. The channel side of the pool can be a convenient starting point for some swimmers, while others prefer to use the wall. Learning to arch your body over the water can be difficult, but most swimmers eventually get it.

EXERCISING THE BACKSTROKE

Swimmers use these drills to focus on specific aspects of their technique before moving to longer swims. All phases of the swim, including hip and shoulder rotation and the recovery and underwater phases of the arm pull, are addressed in these first three drills. The final two exercises improve the swimmer's timing and rhythm.

Backstroke with one arm

Keep one arm relaxed and the other at your side as you swim backward.

Keep the extended arm submerged and the other arm elevated in the final position. When you've kicked for six counts, switch to the other side and do the same with your arms and legs. It's a two-handed backstroke. Swim backward while simultaneously using both arms in this exercise.

Do three one-armed strokes with your right arm, three strokes with alternating arms, and three one-armed strokes with your left arm. Swim two freestyle strokes, then switch to backstroke for two strokes—work on catching and pulling through in the freestyle and backstroke. Increase the number of pulls in the backstroke and freestyle to three or four to make this a new challenge.

During this exercise, pay attention to how the two swims compare in terms of rhythm. With a thumbs-up hand release at the end of each pull, these swimmers are encouraged to finish the pull and get to work. Proper breathing is often overlooked and crucial to stroke tempo when learning the backstroke. Maintain regular and straight inhale and exhalation with stroke even though the nose and mouth are out of the water.

When one arm recovers, the swimmer inhales, and when the other arm recovers, the swimmer exhales through the mouth. In freestyle swimming, the inhale and exhale of this breathing pattern are coordinated with the tempo of the stroke. Practicing backstroke by inhaling through the mouth and exhaling slowly through the nose can help swimmers get used to their breathing. Developing a smooth backstroke rhythm takes time, patience, and a calm mind.

Swimmers can improve their speed using long axis combinations and rhythm exercises.

Techniques for the Backswing

Swimmers' shoulder, leg, and ankle flexibility and overall strength and flexibility all play a role in their choice of backstroke style. At the beginning of a swim, swimmers with more flexible shoulders can angle their palms toward the bottom of the pool, which improves efficiency. Adjustable shoulders help swimmers catch more effectively with less rotation. For swimmers with a limited range of motion, rotating the shoulders slightly and keeping the palms perpendicular to the bottom of the pool can help them improve their stroke.

Although many new swimmers are hesitant to learn or practice any stroke other than freestyle, they should consider adding backstroke to their toolbox. It is possible to improve as a freestyle swimmer by incorporating some backstroke.

Double Arm Backstroke Exercises

The double arm backstroke exercise is a powerful drill designed to enhance a swimmer's coordination, strength, and understanding of the backstroke's rotational dynamics. In backstroke, much like freestyle, the rotation of the hips is a critical component that drives the stroke. Elite swimmers have mastered the ability to maintain an effective rotation angle, which allows them to adjust their pace and power output across various distances.

To perform the double arm backstroke exercise, the swimmer lies on their back and executes both arm strokes simultaneously. This bilateral movement requires a strong core to stabilize the body and prevent excessive rocking. The drill emphasizes the importance of the hips in generating rotational momentum, which is essential for an efficient and powerful backstroke.

An excellent variation of this exercise is the "three pulls plus 12 kicks" drill, which focuses on improving rotational momentum and balance. Here's how it's executed:

Begin by swimming backstroke with both arms moving together in a double arm pull.

After completing three arm pulls, transition into a side-kicking position. Pause in this position and execute 12 full kicks while maintaining a streamlined body alignment. This side-kicking phase reinforces the swimmer's ability to balance and control their rotation.

Following the 12 kicks, resume the double arm backstroke for three more pulls, focusing on a smooth transition between the pulling and kicking phases.

Throughout the exercise, it's crucial to keep the head in a neutral position, with the eyes looking up and slightly forward. This head position helps to maintain a streamlined posture and reduces drag.

As swimmers become proficient in this drill, they will develop a natural inclination to incorporate rotational movements into their backstroke. The body adapts to the angular momentum generated by the hips, making it challenging to swim backstroke without the beneficial side-to-side rotation.

This drill not only improves a swimmer's backstroke technique but also builds endurance and strength in the muscles responsible for rotation. By practicing this exercise regularly, swimmers can expect to see improvements in their speed, efficiency, and overall performance in the backstroke.

Arm backstroke technique for beginners

The elementary backstroke is an essential stroke for beginners to learn as it serves as a foundation for developing comfort and confidence in the water. This stroke is characterized by its simplicity and the ease with which swimmers can keep their faces above water, making it an excellent starting point for those new to swimming.

When teaching the arm technique for the elementary backstroke, it is important to emphasize the importance of a relaxed and streamlined body position. The swimmer should begin by lying flat on their back in the water, with their body extended and their hands resting gently at their sides. This position allows for a moment of rest or glide between strokes, which is crucial for conserving energy and maintaining a smooth rhythm.

To initiate the arm movement, the swimmer should imagine the sides of their body as the seams of a garment. They will then run their fingertips up along these imaginary seams as they raise their arms upward. This motion should be smooth and controlled, with the arms moving in a synchronized manner.

As the arms are raised, the swimmer should focus on keeping their chest open and their hands close to their body. This helps to maintain a streamlined position and reduces drag, allowing for a more efficient glide through the water.

To practice the arm movement on land and improve flexibility and balance, the swimmer can lie on the floor or a bed. This dryland exercise allows the swimmer to focus on the path of their arms without the added complexity of being in the water. It also serves to stretch and strengthen the triceps muscles, which are crucial for the pulling phase of the stroke.

Additionally, the swimmer can sit on a chair to simulate the prone (face down) and supine (face up) positions used in swimming. This practice helps to reinforce proper body alignment and the coordination of arm movements with the rest of the body.

The elementary backstroke is not only a valuable skill for beginners but also a therapeutic exercise that can be used for relaxation and gentle muscle conditioning. By mastering the arm technique and understanding the importance of body position and movement, swimmers can build a solid foundation for learning more advanced strokes in the future.

Backstroke with a flutter kick for beginners

The backstroke with a flutter kick is a fundamental skill for beginner swimmers to master, as it lays the groundwork for a strong and efficient backstroke. The flutter kick is a continuous, alternating motion that provides propulsion while the body is positioned on the back. When teaching beginners, it's important to break down the stroke into manageable parts, focusing on body position, arm movement, and the flutter kick.

To start, encourage swimmers to become comfortable with the sensation of moving backward in the water. They can practice this by walking backward in the shallow end, which helps them get used to the idea of propulsion in the opposite direction of their gaze. As they walk, they should focus on keeping their back slightly arched, which mimics the body position needed for backstroke.

Once comfortable with moving backward, introduce the flutter kick. The swimmer should practice this kick while holding onto the pool edge or a kickboard to isolate the movement. The flutter kick originates from the hips, with the legs straight and the toes pointed. The motion is a quick, up-and-down movement with minimal bend in the knees. Encourage swimmers to keep their kicks small and consistent, which will help maintain a steady rhythm and prevent them from tiring too quickly.

After mastering the flutter kick, it's time to add the elementary backstroke arm movement. This movement is characterized by the "tick-tock-toy" sequence: the hands move from the hips ('tick'), up to the armpits ('tock'), and then extend outwards and together above the head ('toy'). This arm stroke is synchronized with the flutter kick to create a smooth and continuous motion.

As beginners gain confidence, they can start to reduce the amount of support they use, such as letting go of the pool edge or kickboard. They can initiate the stroke with either the arm movement or the flutter kick, depending on which feels more natural to them. It's important to make gradual adjustments to ensure they do not become overwhelmed by trying to coordinate too many movements at once.

When practicing the full stroke, swimmers should focus on maintaining a consistent flutter kick and a smooth arm stroke. They should also pay attention to their head position, keeping their head still and their gaze upward. This will help them maintain a straight line in the water and reduce drag.

By breaking down the backstroke into these components and practicing each one individually before combining them, beginner swimmers will develop a sense of strength and fluidity in their strokes. With patience and practice, they will be amazed at the progress they can make in both their technique and their confidence in the water.

Windmill backstroke

The windmill backstroke is an advanced variation of the traditional backstroke that emphasizes a continuous, circular arm motion akin to the blades of a windmill. This technique can enhance the swimmer's propulsion and rhythm in the water. To master the windmill backstroke, it's crucial to develop a smooth, flowing motion that allows for efficient swimming on the back.

Begin by familiarizing yourself with the supine position, which is the foundational posture for backstroke swimming. To transition into this position, lean back and push off from the bottom of the pool with your feet, ensuring that your toes are pointed and your feet are close to the water's surface. This streamlined position reduces drag and allows for a more efficient kick.

As you become comfortable with the supine position, focus on maintaining a gentle, continuous flutter kick. The flutter kick is performed by alternating your legs in a quick, up-and-down motion, originating from the hips with minimal knee bend. The toes should remain pointed, and the feet should break the surface of the water slightly, creating a small splash. This kick helps to keep your body level and stable as you swim.

When incorporating the windmill arm motion, it's important to coordinate the arms so that as one arm enters the water above the head, the other arm is exiting the water by the hip. The arms should move in a large, circular pattern, with the hand entering the water little finger first to reduce resistance. The arm motion should be fluid and continuous, with no pause at any point in the cycle.

Pay particular attention to the inner thighs during the kick. Engaging the inner thigh muscles helps to keep the legs together and streamlines the body, which is essential for maintaining balance and reducing drag. The combination of a strong flutter kick and the windmill arm motion will propel you through the water with speed and efficiency.

As you practice the windmill backstroke, remember to keep your head still and your gaze directed upwards. This will help you maintain a straight line in the water and ensure that your body does not rotate excessively, which can disrupt the rhythm of your stroke.

In summary, the windmill backstroke is a dynamic and powerful stroke that requires practice and coordination. By focusing on the supine position, maintaining a consistent flutter kick, and executing a smooth windmill arm motion, swimmers can develop a backstroke technique that is both effective and graceful. With dedication and proper technique, the windmill backstroke can be a valuable addition to any swimmer's skill set.

Flutter Kick in the Backstroke of a Windmill

The fundamental windmill backstroke is now complete. After a brief rest, the right arm begins to catch the ball with its left arm. Assume a prone position and start your workout.

Once the arm moves down, work on getting the push-off down. Standing in the back with a partner and supporting yourself in the train driver positions, releasing and holding hands as they strike, is an option if you require assistance. Without a training partner, you can support yourself by doing the flutter and backstroke with your free arm while sliding your other hand along the pool's edge. It's wise to keep the water level at ear level by keeping your chin near your chest and looking toward your feet.

To raise one's backstroke height

To elevate the efficiency and effectiveness of your backstroke, it is essential to focus on optimizing your body position and rotation in the water. A well-executed backstroke not only enhances your hydrodynamic profile but also can effectively increase your height in the water by several centimeters. This elevated position reduces drag and allows for a more powerful and propulsive stroke.

To achieve this, concentrate on maintaining a strong, stable core and a streamlined body position. Your head should be in a neutral position, with your eyes looking straight up and your ears submerged. This posture helps to lift your hips and legs to the surface, minimizing resistance against the water.

Body rotation is a critical component of an efficient backstroke. It should be initiated from the core, with your shoulders and hips rotating together as a single unit. This rotation allows for a longer reach and a more forceful pull, which in turn can increase your propulsion. Aim for a smooth and continuous rotational movement, with each shoulder rolling to initiate the arm's catch phase in the water.

Monitoring your stroke count per length is a valuable tool to gauge your progress. As you refine your technique and build strength, you may notice a reduction in the number of strokes needed to cover a given distance. This indicates improved efficiency and control over your movements in the water.

When it comes to the speed of your hand movement, it's important to synchronize it with the overall tempo of your body. During the catch phase, your hand should enter the water gently and then gradually accelerate through the pull phase. This acceleration should be controlled and not rushed. By the time your hand exits the water at the end of the stroke, it should be moving at its fastest to maximize propulsion.

Remember, the goal is not to simply move your hands faster, but to increase the force applied during the pull phase while maintaining a steady and sustainable rhythm. This nuanced approach to hand speed and stroke rate will contribute to a more powerful and efficient backstroke.

By focusing on body position, core rotation, and a progressive hand speed that matches the body's velocity, you can elevate your backstroke technique. Keep track of your stroke count, and strive for a balance between power and grace in the water. With dedicated practice and attention to these details, you will see marked improvements in your backstroke performance.

FREESTYLE

Freestyle, often referred to as the front crawl, is widely recognized for its efficiency and speed, making it a staple in competitive swimming. In freestyle events, swimmers are granted the freedom to choose any stroke, but the front crawl is predominantly used due to its superior velocity. It is characterized by the alternate overhand motion of the arms and the flutter kick of the legs.

In a 50-meter freestyle race, while it is technically permissible to swim butterfly, backstroke, or breaststroke, it is strategically advantageous to utilize the front crawl unless a swimmer has a specific tactical reason not to, such as achieving an official qualification time in another stroke.

Transitioning to backstroke, this stroke shares the principle of body rotation with freestyle, but it is executed on the swimmer's back. The rotation occurs around the body's longitudinal axis, engaging the core muscles and alleviating stress on the shoulders. An efficient backstroke begins with a proficient catch, where the hand enters the water and sets up for a powerful pull. The underwater pull phase should be executed with a swift hand movement, maintaining a high elbow position to maximize the power phase.

The point of entry for the hand varies among swimmers, largely due to shoulder flexibility. Typically, the hand should enter the water between 8 to 12 inches deep, with the palm facing outwards and the shoulder reaching forward to extend the arm fully.

The concept of swimming from the hips is crucial for both

freestyle and backstroke. Effective body rotation is essential for an efficient pull in these strokes. Swimmers who master this technique often require fewer strokes to cover a 50-meter distance. Conversely, swimmers with a less stable core may exhibit a fishtail motion or excessive lateral hip movement, which creates drag and diminishes efficiency.

During the backstroke pull, the body should be positioned to minimize drag at the lowest point of the grip, while the shoulder should emerge at the highest point. The underside of the arm, including the hand and forearm, should maintain consistent pressure on the water throughout the pull phase.

To optimize the pull, swimmers may adjust their elbow bend during the underwater phase, bringing the hand closer to the body towards the end of the pull. This adjustment can enhance the propulsion and streamline the recovery of the arm.

The "hand to foot" time is a metric used to measure the duration from when the hand enters the water on the final stroke before the turn to when the feet make contact with the wall during the turn. This timing is critical for maximizing the efficiency of turns and maintaining momentum throughout the race.

In summary, both freestyle and backstroke benefit from a strong core, effective body rotation, and precise technique in the catch and pull phases. By focusing on these elements, swimmers can improve their efficiency and speed in the water.

CRAWL

In freestyle swimming, the most common kicking patterns are the two-beat, four-beat, and six-beat kicks. Each of these kicking rhythms serves a distinct purpose and is chosen based on the swimmer's strategy, distance of the race, and personal strengths.

The two-beat kick is a relaxed and energy-efficient pattern where the swimmer performs one kick per arm cycle. This kick is particularly favored by distance swimmers, including those competing in open water and triathlons. The reduced kicking frequency conserves energy, which is crucial for long-distance events where endurance is key.

The four-beat kick strikes a balance between propulsion and energy conservation. It involves two kicks per arm cycle, offering a bit more stability and speed than the two-beat kick without significantly increasing energy expenditure. This kick can be useful for middle-distance events or for swimmers who prefer a slightly faster tempo without the intensity of a sprint.

The six-beat kick is the most vigorous of the three, with three kicks per arm cycle. This high-tempo kick provides maximum propulsion and stability, making it the preferred choice for sprinters who need to generate the greatest speed over short distances. The six-beat kick helps maintain a high body position in the water and contributes to a powerful forward thrust, but it is also the most energy-intensive.

It's essential for swimmers to choose a kicking pattern that aligns with their race strategy and physical capabilities. For example, a sprinter specializing in the 50-meter freestyle may benefit from the six-beat kick's propulsive power, while a swimmer tackling a 10-kilometer open water race would likely opt for the energy efficiency of the two-beat kick.

The freestyle stroke is versatile, and its variations in kicking patterns allow swimmers to tailor their technique to the specific demands of their events. Mastery of these different rhythms can lead to improved performance, whether the goal is speed in a sprint or endurance in a marathon swim.

Free swimming exercises

Masters swimmers, who often seek to refine their technique and enhance their performance, can benefit greatly from a tailored set of drills. These exercises are designed to hone in on the critical elements of freestyle swimming, such as body alignment, stroke length, breathing patterns, the catch, the pull phase, and arm recovery. For those swimmers whose kick may not be their strongest asset, the use of fins can provide the necessary propulsion, allowing them to focus on upper body mechanics.

One effective drill to improve coordination and timing is the one-arm freestyle. Beginning in a streamlined position, with both arms extended above the head, the swimmer initiates the stroke with one arm while leaving the other extended. This isolates the movement of each arm, allowing the swimmer to concentrate on the nuances of the stroke cycle with greater clarity.

Breathing should be integrated seamlessly into the stroke. A swift inhalation is followed by a return to a neutral head position, eyes cast down to the bottom of the pool. It's crucial to avoid holding one's breath, as this can lead to a buildup of carbon dioxide and subsequent discomfort.

Throughout the pull phase, maintaining a streamlined body position is essential. As the hand enters the catch position, the body should rotate along its longitudinal axis, enhancing the efficiency of the pull. This rotation is a key component of the freestyle stroke, as it allows for a longer reach and a more powerful propulsion.

The one-arm drill can be modified to resemble the catch-up stroke, where one arm waits for the other to complete its cycle before initiating its own stroke. This variation emphasizes the importance of timing and coordination between arms.

Championship swimmers often recommend practicing freestyle with clenched fists. This drill forces swimmers to focus on using their forearms during the pull phase, thereby improving their feel for the water and increasing the efficiency of their stroke.

A clean and precise arm recovery sets the stage for an optimal hand entry. Visualize your hand piercing the water's surface at a point directly in front of your shoulder, thumb or middle finger first, followed by the forearm and elbow. This entry minimizes drag and positions the arm for an effective pull.

To maximize the length of the underwater stroke, extend your fingertips forward as far as possible without compromising body alignment. One arm should be fully extended underwater, while the other recovers above the water with the shoulder, elbow, and hand positioned to minimize resistance and prepare for the next entry.

These drills are not meant to be used continuously throughout a workout but rather during specific sets focused on technique. Swimmers with good shoulder, leg, and ankle flexibility will find the most success, as they can fully utilize the shoulder rotation and achieve a strong push-off.

When practicing shoulder-driven freestyle, the emphasis is on accelerating the arm recovery in conjunction with a butterfly kick. This style is characterized by a rapid tempo and is best practiced over short distances with ample rest intervals to ensure the preservation of technique. It's a style that prioritizes speed and power over endurance, making it an excellent choice for sprint training.

THE BUTTERFLY

The butterfly stroke is a symphony of power and grace, a stroke that epitomizes the fusion of strength and technique in the sport of swimming. Its evolution from the breaststroke was a game-changer in competitive swimming, and the term "butterfly" aptly describes the undulating motion that characterizes this dynamic stroke.

The genesis of the butterfly stroke can be traced back to swimmers who discovered that they could propel themselves faster through the water by recovering their arms over the surface, rather than pushing them forward underwater as in traditional breaststroke. This innovation led to the distinctive arm movement that resembles the flapping of a butterfly's wings, hence the name.
For novice butterfly swimmers, mastering the stroke's rhythm and mechanics can be challenging. One common error is to rush through the stroke cycle without fully extending the body, applying pressure on the chest, or allowing for a brief pause to set up the catch properly. A well-executed catch is crucial for generating a powerful and efficient butterfly stroke.

The catch in butterfly, much like in freestyle, requires swimmers to maintain a high elbow position while their fingertips, hands, and forearms press down and outwards to effectively "grip" the water. This action sets the stage for the propulsive phase of the stroke. The "corner" refers to the hand position at the widest part of the catch phase, where the hands are fully extended and ready to initiate the pull.

As the arms pull through the water, swimmers must maintain the high elbow position, drawing their hands back towards the body while keeping them in front of the abdomen. This motion is akin to tracing the outline of a keyhole with the hands, ensuring that the propulsion is directed backwards rather than downwards, which would otherwise lift the body but not move it forward.

The underwater phase of the butterfly stroke is a delicate balance of power and positioning. As the hands and forearms accelerate from the controlled catch to the more forceful push, the chest undulates from its lowest point in the wave to its highest just before breaking the surface. This wave-like motion is essential for maintaining the stroke's momentum and facilitating the recovery phase, where the arms sweep over the water to return to the starting position.

Timing is everything in butterfly. The seamless integration of the underwater pull with the overwater recovery is what allows swimmers to maintain a rhythmic and sustainable stroke. Beginners often struggle with the recovery phase, sometimes trapping their hands too close to the body at the end of the pull, which can disrupt the stroke's flow and lead to early fatigue.

To illustrate, consider Michael Phelps, an exemplary butterfly swimmer whose technique showcases the importance of a well-timed catch and recovery. Phelps' ability to maintain a high elbow position throughout the stroke and execute a fluid recovery is a testament to his mastery of the butterfly's intricate mechanics.

DOLPHIN KICK

At the heart of the butterfly stroke is the dolphin kick, which is the foundation for the undulating body movement characteristic of the stroke. The kick originates from the core, with the movement flowing like a wave through the body to the tips of the toes. This motion is synchronized with the arm strokes to create a continuous and fluid movement through the water.

For beginners, mastering the dolphin kick and its timing in relation to the arm strokes can be daunting. However, when the timing and body rhythm are synchronized, the butterfly stroke can be performed with a sense of effortlessness. The swimmer does not have to consciously think about each component of the stroke; instead, it becomes a natural and rhythmic cycle.

The upper body initiates the stroke with the arms entering the water in front of the head, thumbs first, and extending forward. As the hands press down and out in a keyhole pattern, the chest presses down, and the hips rise in response to the first half of the dolphin kick. This is followed by a powerful whip of the legs, propelling the swimmer forward and aiding in the recovery of the arms.

The timing of the dolphin kick is critical. The first kick occurs as the hands enter the water, helping to balance the body and maintain a streamlined position. The second kick takes place as the arms sweep out of the water, providing additional propulsion and momentum for the recovery phase.

To visualize this, imagine a swimmer like Michael Phelps, whose butterfly technique is a testament to the beauty and efficiency of the stroke. Phelps' seamless integration of the dolphin kick with his arm strokes exemplifies the perfect rhythm that all butterfly swimmers aspire to achieve.

In practice, swimmers should focus on developing a strong core to support the undulating motion of the dolphin kick. Drills that isolate the kick, such as using a kickboard or performing vertical dolphin kicks, can help swimmers build the necessary muscle memory and strength.

Additionally, timing the breath to coincide with the natural rise of the chest during the stroke cycle is essential. The swimmer should aim to breathe every one or two strokes, turning the head to the side just before the arms recover over the water.

In summary, the butterfly stroke is a harmonious blend of power, grace, and timing. It requires a swimmer to engage the entire body, from the fingertips to the toes, in a rhythmic and coordinated movement. With practice and attention to the nuances of the stroke, swimmers can develop a butterfly that is both propulsive and efficient, allowing them to glide through the water with the elegance of its namesake.

One arm only

Hold one arm at your side and do a butterfly stroke with the other arm, breathing to the side of the flapping arm. This is a helpful way to improve the timing and rhythm of your swim. It helps you keep your arm straight. Combining the underwater phase of the swim with the recovery phase is possible.

Move quickly through the final stroke and into the recovery phase. This popular exercise to promote rhythm and timing begins with the push-off from the wall. The underwater dolphin kick can be performed with your hands at your sides or with your arms above your head. Focus on working your abdominal and lower back muscles to direct energy flow through your hips and legs. Do this while flicking your feet at the end of the kick.

SAM HUMPHRIES

Successful underwater dolphin swimmers do not move their chest or arms very much. Kick upward and push off with your feet just below the water's surface.

BUTTERFLY KICK EXERCISE

The butterfly kick is a fundamental component of the butterfly stroke, and mastering its rhythm is crucial for efficiency and speed in the water. To enhance the feel for this rhythm, one effective exercise involves focusing on a single arm stroke while adopting a modified freestyle arm motion for the recovery phase. This drill simplifies the stroke, allowing the swimmer to concentrate on the timing and power of the kick.

During this exercise, one arm remains extended forward in a neutral position, cutting through the water and providing stability. The other arm performs the complete butterfly stroke, from the pull through to the recovery. As the working arm sweeps through the water, the swimmer breathes to the side, similar to a freestyle stroke, which can be less taxing and more natural for some swimmers.

This drill not only helps in isolating the kick and its timing with the arm stroke but also encourages the swimmer to maintain a continuous and rhythmic motion, akin to the natural undulation of a dolphin. By focusing on one arm at a time, swimmers can pay closer attention to the subtleties of their technique, such as the positioning of their hands and the engagement of their core muscles.

Training short axis strokes like the butterfly can be optimized by breaking down the stroke into segments. Incorporating a freestyle kick into butterfly training is an advanced technique that can yield significant improvements. This combination encourages a more vigorous butterfly stroke by emphasizing the underwater power phase. The freestyle kick helps to flatten out the body position, which can lead to a faster stroke tempo and a more streamlined form.

By practicing the butterfly stroke with a freestyle kick, swimmers can develop greater strength and endurance in their kick, which translates to a more powerful and efficient butterfly stroke. This drill also offers variety in training, which can prevent mental and physical fatigue, keeping workouts engaging and productive.

The butterfly kick exercise with a single-arm stroke and freestyle recovery is a strategic approach to refining the butterfly rhythm. It allows swimmers to dissect their stroke, focus on the power and timing of their kick, and ultimately build a stronger, more efficient butterfly stroke.

FASTER BUTTERFLY

To swim faster in butterfly, it is essential to optimize the body's line in the water, much like in freestyle. This concept involves extending the body fully with each stroke, creating a streamlined form that reduces drag and maximizes forward propulsion.

When we discuss lengthening the body line, we are referring to the elongation of the body from the tips of the fingers to the toes. In butterfly, as the arms enter the water, the fingertips should be the leading edge, setting the direction for the rest of the body to follow. As the hands enter, the chest naturally presses down in a wave-like motion, which is a key element of the butterfly's undulating rhythm.

This pressing of the chest not only helps to lengthen the body but also initiates the powerful underwater pull. The hands and forearms should catch the water and push it backwards, propelling the swimmer forward. It is during this phase that the body follows the path of the fingertips, as the hands move from the catch phase into the press and eventual release at the hips.
The ingrained pattern of movement mentioned refers to the muscle memory developed through consistent practice. The more a swimmer repeats the correct motion, the more natural it becomes, allowing for greater efficiency and speed in the water.

For example, consider the technique of Olympic champion Michael Phelps. His butterfly stroke is characterized by a high elbow catch and a body line that extends forward with each stroke, minimizing resistance and maximizing the power of his pull and kick. Phelps' body follows a precise and practiced path through the water, a result of countless hours perfecting his technique.

To swim faster in butterfly, focus on extending the body line with each pull, ensuring that the fingertips lead the way, and the chest presses down to facilitate a powerful and efficient stroke. This approach, combined with a strong and rhythmic kick, will help swimmers cut through the water with speed and grace.

HOW TO GET RID OF RESISTANCE IN THE BUTTERFLY

One of the most critical factors to consider is the reduction of resistance. Water, being nearly 800 times denser than air, presents a significant challenge to swimmers. Unlike fish, which have evolved streamlined bodies to slip through water with minimal resistance, humans must rely on technique to overcome this natural barrier. The concept of resistance in swimming is multifaceted, encompassing both drag and the swimmer's ability to effectively transfer energy into propulsion.

When a swimmer's body moves through water, it creates turbulence, which can increase drag and decrease the efficiency of their movements. To mitigate this, swimmers must focus on maintaining a streamlined position in the water, minimizing the surface area that leads their movement and thus reducing the drag force. In the butterfly stroke, the swimmer's body undulates in a wave-like motion, which, when executed correctly, can help to maintain a streamlined form.

However, any unnecessary movement or misalignment can increase turbulence and drag, making it harder to move through the water. This is why the swimmer cannot simply add more energy to overcome the resistance; doing so in turbulent water would only exacerbate the inefficiency. To illustrate, let's consider the example of a fish versus a human swimmer.

Fish are naturally adapted to their aquatic environment, with bodies that are designed for efficient movement through water. Their muscle structure, skin texture, and overall shape allow them to reach impressive speeds, with some species capable of swimming up to 50 kilometers per hour. In contrast, even the fastest human swimmers reach speeds of only about five kilometers per hour. This stark difference is due to the human body's less hydrodynamic shape and the fact that swimmers must work against the water's resistance with every stroke. Elite swimmers like Michael Phelps or Caeleb Dressel have honed their technique to maximize their power transfer and minimize resistance, but the physical limitations remain.

To reduce resistance in the butterfly stroke, swimmers should focus on several key elements:

Body Position: Keep the body as horizontal as possible, with a strong core to maintain alignment.

Undulation: The wave-like body movement should originate from the chest and flow through the hips, with minimal vertical movement.

Arm Entry: Hands should enter the water in line with the shoulders and extend forward smoothly to maintain a streamlined position.

Kick: The dolphin kick should be powerful yet compact, with the feet snapping together to push water directly behind the swimmer.

By refining these aspects of the butterfly stroke, swimmers can achieve a more efficient transfer of energy, propelling themselves through the water with greater speed and less effort. It is the mastery of these techniques, rather than brute force, that allows swimmers to approach their maximum potential in the water.

BREASTSTROKE

The undulating breaststroke was developed by a Hungarian coach in the late 1980s and early 1990s. The breaststroke, which they learned in their youth, is preferred by many master swimmers. Most adult swimmers prefer the wave style because it makes them faster and more efficient. These two styles of swimming are referred to as "short stroke" styles because swimmers turn on the short axis of the body through the hips. Instruction is similar to the butterfly. It begins with the push-off, moves to the arms, and concludes with integrating all components into a whole.

The breaststroke is a great swimming style for some. Other swimming styles have overtaken breaststroke in speed and efficiency over the last 200 years due to advances in swimming techniques.

In butterfly and backstroke, the upper body rotates with the hips as the horizontal axis point rather than the central axis running from the head through the spine. Breaststroke is the slowest swimming style because the upper body rotates in short-distance swimming and the body position is deeper in the water. Since we are deeper in the water in breaststroke, we must address our body position first. As you breathe, your hips sink into the deepest part of the stroke, slowing you down.

In breaststroke, each stroke begins and ends in this position. Remember that your goal in breaststroke is to keep your body position as high as possible during all phases of the pull. This is sometimes the only thing you see in a competitive swim, unlike others.

The push-off is critical to butterfly performance, and you should incorporate drills to develop a solid and symmetrical push-off, meaning you emphasize the downstroke and the upstroke of the push-off. Breaststroke-specific exercises target muscles throughout the torso and legs to help the body glide and undulate through the water. Rowing movements support both swimming styles. Rowing drills consider the different ranges of motion and arm positions relative to the body that occur during swimming strokes.

On the toes

The breaststroke begins by bringing your heels back far enough to touch your hands while swimming on your back. At the end of each repetition, you should perform a gliding motion, similar to the different phases of the breaststroke. Bring the heels "up" toward the butt, then turn the heels "out" by rotating the heels "around and together" to the starting position. Think "up, out, around, and together" with each kick.

A variation of this exercise is to keep your arms in a streamlined position while floating on your back or stomach. The breaststroke can be practiced most effectively while lying on your back.

Take-off

After the start and after each turn, the swimming rules allow a breaststroke pullout. The pullout provides a long pull path back to the legs and enables athletes to flow through the deep blue without causing turbulence. There is no limit to how far a swimmer can go underwater. Elite swimmers cover a distance of 8-10 meters at the turnaround and surface to begin swimming.

The most talented swimmers in the world do this before tensing their muscles. The dolphin kick and arm pull to keep you underwater.

If you are smart about your training, you can swim faster. Swimming with a high body position, proper stroke technique, and high intensity on the short axes is essential. In contrast, freestyle and backstroke are still easy to master without compromising timing or accuracy.

Focus on training with the proper stroke length and intensity. I recommend focusing on shorter distances, higher reps, and longer rests when training for the breaststroke. If you want to swim 300 breaststrokes in one session, break it up into 6 x 50 seconds.

When learning a faster breaststroke, the goal is always to execute the stroke with optimal technique and intensity that mimics the desired result.

In breaststroke, the core movements, posture, and timing have been modified in a constant effort to minimize drag. Breaststroke is the only swimming style in which swimmers push the water forward with their arms and legs during the recovery cycle, resulting in massive drag and deceleration.

The push and pull pattern

The curved push and pull paths create propulsion. The breaststroke is three-dimensional and serves as the sole source of propulsion for half of the swim cycle. The breaststroke stroke consists of two phases. The other strokes are pulled and pushed simultaneously.

Breaststroke swimmers begin each stroke cycle in a streamlined position with arms and head below the water surface. Assuming a proper catch position depends on the outhaul motion.

Swimmers make a circular motion with their feet out, back, and down to begin and end the breaststroke stroke.

The feet of the fastest breaststroke swimmers push back into the water as long as possible. The swimmer can extend his limbs if his feet are wide enough. Swimmers achieve high forward speeds by controlling their pull and push path. Their efforts are severely compromised if they do not use tip techniques to propel the limbs forward.

Elite breaststroke swimmers control core movement and stroke timing to minimize the severity and duration of deceleration during arm and leg recovery. This striking feature is one of the reasons for the significant time loss in breaststroke. Breaststroke swimmers had to shorten their arms and torso to get the most out of their legs.

Breaststroke with push-off

The pull generates more force than the push-off. The body encounters more resistance when moving faster than at any other time in the swim cycle. Getting everything in front of your hips during the push-off is essential. If you want to swim more quickly in the breaststroke, you need to increase the tempo of your short axis rotation.

In the breaststroke, if you move your chest down and forward faster after you inhale, your hands will come tighter to their anchor point. This is because you are more quickly ready for the next powerful torso contraction that brings your hips to the anchor point.

Performing the breaststroke exercise

The exercise consists of a breaststroke cycle with two kicks, one pull, and two lifts. Swing out and start a new stroke after staying in the current for two full kicks. Two down, one up. This conditioning exercise requires you to complete a full breaststroke cycle and stay underwater for more streamlined pulls.

Breaststroke with Dolphin Kick

At the heart of the butterfly stroke is the dolphin kick, which is the foundation for the undulating body movement characteristic of the stroke. The kick originates from the core, with the movement flowing like a wave through the body to the tips of the toes. This motion is synchronized with the arm strokes to create a continuous and fluid movement through the water.

For beginners, mastering the dolphin kick and its timing in relation to the arm strokes can be daunting. However, when the timing and body rhythm are synchronized, the butterfly stroke can be performed with a sense of effortlessness. The swimmer does not have to consciously think about each component of the stroke; instead, it becomes a natural and rhythmic cycle.

The upper body initiates the stroke with the arms entering the water in front of the head, thumbs first, and extending forward. As the hands press down and out in a keyhole pattern, the chest presses down, and the hips rise in response to the first half of the dolphin kick. This is followed by a powerful whip of the legs, propelling the swimmer forward and aiding in the recovery of the arms.

The timing of the dolphin kick is critical. The first kick occurs as the hands enter the water, helping to balance the body and maintain a streamlined position. The second kick takes place as the arms sweep out of the water, providing additional propulsion and momentum for the recovery phase.

To visualize this, imagine a swimmer like Michael Phelps, whose butterfly technique is a testament to the beauty and efficiency of the stroke. Phelps' seamless integration of the dolphin kick with his arm strokes exemplifies the perfect rhythm that all butterfly swimmers aspire to achieve.

In practice, swimmers should focus on developing a strong core to support the undulating motion of the dolphin kick. Drills that isolate the kick, such as using a kickboard or performing vertical dolphin kicks, can help swimmers build the necessary muscle memory and strength.
Additionally, timing the breath to coincide with the natural rise of the chest during the stroke cycle is essential. The swimmer should aim to breathe every one or two strokes, turning the head to the side just before the arms recover over the water.

The butterfly stroke is a harmonious blend of power, grace, and timing. It requires a swimmer to engage the entire body, from the fingertips to the toes, in a rhythmic and coordinated movement. With practice and attention to the nuances of the stroke, swimmers can develop a butterfly that is both propulsive and efficient, allowing them to glide through the water with the elegance of its namesake.

In the recovery phase of breaststroke, pull your heels toward your buttocks. To minimize resistance, hide your legs behind your hips and torso in the first phase. Keep your knees and thighs together while your feet point backward to keep your body streamlined. Typically, the push-off begins when breaststroke beginners pull their knees under their bodies, breaking the body line.

This habit is tough to correct when you practice breaststroke with a kickboard. Once you understand the basic mechanics of breaststroke, you can practice it independently. The water at the top of the lunge can be touched with your feet. Turn the toes outward so the soles and arches of the feet can touch the water. Bend the toes toward the knees and place the heels just below the water's surface.

Keep the knees together as you catch, but move the feet away from the body line to hold more water. You can feel the pressure of the water on the inside of your feet. Regardless of the width of the kick, it is vital to hold the water with your legs. Stretch your legs straight out, and your feet engage the water in the final stage of the buoyancy.

Keep the heels below the water line when you want to push the feet back in an elliptical shape. Use the tops of your feet and your inner leg muscles to push the water back and forth. At the end of the kick, close your feet by clapping the arches of your feet together. It looks and feels like you have catapulted forward as you have a positive connection between your feet and the water.

BREASTSTROKE KICK

The swimmer starts in a prone position, with the body horizontal and the arms extended forward in a streamlined position. The kick begins by bending the knees and bringing the heels towards the buttocks. The feet then turn outward, and the swimmer presses the soles of their feet against the water, pushing backward and outward in a circular motion. The legs then snap together to complete the kick, propelling the swimmer forward.

During the breaststroke kick, it is crucial to maintain a narrow kick to avoid excessive drag. The knees should not separate widely or break the surface of the water. The upper body remains still, with the head in line with the spine, and the arms execute a simultaneous pull that complements the kick.

When practicing the breaststroke kick with a pull buoy, the swimmer should focus on maintaining a compact and powerful kick without allowing the knees to come too close to the surface. The buoy helps to keep the hips elevated, which is essential for a proper breaststroke body position.

In both strokes, the body should undulate slightly but remain mostly horizontal, with the hips near the surface. Tension in the body should be minimized to avoid resistance and ensure efficient movement through the water.

By focusing on the distinct techniques of the backstroke flutter kick and the breaststroke frog kick, swimmers can develop the specific skills necessary to excel in each stroke.

TAKE A DIRECT LINE OF ATTACK UNDERWATER

Underwater Streamline

The underwater streamline is a fundamental skill in competitive swimming that allows swimmers to take advantage of the reduced drag underwater to maximize their speed off the starts and turns. When executing the underwater streamline, the swimmer should extend their arms straight over their head, one hand on top of the other, with biceps pressed against the ears. The body should be as tight and elongated as possible, forming a torpedo-like shape to cut through the water efficiently.

Integration of the Kick

While maintaining this streamlined position, swimmers engage in a dolphin kick in butterfly, backstroke, and freestyle. The dolphin kick involves undulating the body from the chest to the toes in a wave-like motion, with the power generated from the core and hips. The legs should remain together, with the feet pointed to optimize the kick's effectiveness.

In contrast, the breaststroke requires a different underwater phase known as the pullout. After the start or turn, the swimmer is allowed one arm pull followed by one breaststroke kick while remaining underwater. The hands should be stretched forward into a streamline position after the pull and before the kick.

Transition to Surface Swimming

To transition smoothly from the underwater phase to surface swimming, the swimmer must time their kicks and begin to angle upwards as they approach the 15-meter mark, where they are required to surface. The last few kicks should increase in power to help the swimmer break the surface with momentum.

Masters Swimmers and Efficient Turns
Masters swimmers, even if not competing in organized meets, can benefit greatly from practicing efficient turns and underwater work. By focusing on a powerful push-off from the wall and maintaining a tight streamline position, they can conserve energy and increase their speed in the water. The goal is to carry the speed from the push-off into the swimming strokes, whether it's freestyle, backstroke, butterfly, or breaststroke.

Maximizing Speed from the Start
Swimmers indeed achieve their top speed within moments of leaping from the starting block. The explosive power of the legs, combined with a streamlined entry into the water, allows swimmers to enter at high velocity. Maintaining this speed through a strong underwater phase and a seamless transition to surface swimming is crucial for a fast start.

By focusing on these elements—streamline position, integration of the kick, transition to surface swimming, and efficient turns—swimmers can significantly improve their performance in the water. Whether for competitive racing or fitness swimming, mastering these techniques can lead to more efficient and faster swimming.

LEARN TO DIVE IN A POOL APPROVED FOR COMPETITIVE DIVING

When instructing swimmers on the art of diving, it is imperative to emphasize safety and proper technique. Diving should always be practiced in a pool that is approved for competitive diving, where the depth is adequate to prevent injury. The ideal location for diving is in the deep end of the pool, where there is at least 15 feet of open water. This allows the swimmer to glide and submerge safely without the risk of encountering the bottom too soon. It is crucial to avoid diving in the shallow end, as it often contains ledges and slopes that can pose a serious risk to swimmers.

The use of standardized whistles and commands during practice is beneficial as it helps swimmers concentrate on their performance after leaving the starting block. A clear and consistent signal allows swimmers to mentally prepare for the dive and execute it with precision.

Just as a golfer works on refining their swing, swimmers must pay close attention to the nuances of their strokes. Stroke drills are an excellent tool for this purpose and should be incorporated into practice sessions. These drills allow swimmers to isolate and focus on specific aspects of their stroke, such as hand entry, body rotation, or kick timing. By repeatedly practicing these drills, swimmers can integrate the refined technique into their natural stroke pattern.

For example, a swimmer looking to improve their freestyle stroke might focus on a drill that emphasizes a high elbow catch, ensuring that they are pulling water efficiently. Over time, with consistent practice, this improved catch becomes an integral part of the swimmer's freestyle, leading to a more effective and faster stroke.

It is important to remember that changes to stroke technique can take time to become ingrained. Swimmers should be patient and persistent, understanding that the integration of a new skill or modification to their stroke will gradually become second nature with dedicated practice. Coaches should encourage swimmers to maintain focus on these details, as they are the building blocks of a proficient and competitive swimming technique.

THE FLUTTER KICK

It is an undulating motion that starts in the hip joints, goes through the legs, and ends with a whipping motion of the feet. Some freestyle kicks that master swimmers use are more efficient than others. New swimmers tend to initiate the lift from the knees, increasing resistance and affecting their body position. Swimmers should do everything they can to maximize the benefits and minimize the effort required for the kicks by incorporating agility training into their workouts.

Keep your hips on the water's surface by pushing your neck down. If you raise your head, your hips will sink. So resist the temptation to tilt your chin. Generally, backstroke swimmers maintain a steady six-stroke rhythm with a strong push-off throughout the swim. Many backstroke coaches believe that a good push-off leads to proper posture, which in turn allows for a smooth catch and more power.

You should perform a small and steady kick to relax your jaw and neck muscles. Lifting your knees in a cycling motion will affect your posture and cause additional resistance. Swimmers can improve their technique by increasing the flexibility of their hip flexors and using fins.

Building an efficient backstroke can be achieved by using postural and push-off exercises. By tensing your abdominal muscles, you keep your spine neutral. Your body rotates toward your outstretched arm, lowering your shoulder and lifting the opposite shoulder out of the water while keeping your head neutral. Keep your extended arm against your head to tighten your body.

Swimmers with high shoulder flexibility should keep their arms in a streamlined position above their heads. To avoid arching your back, you need to strengthen your abdominal muscles. Keep the push-off as short as possible. Master swimmers with limited ankle mobility can use fins to improve their push-off mechanics during drills.

Adult swimmers push off too much because they feel their legs give way. The push-off is not only listless and energy-sapping, but it also prevents a fluid swim. The ideal push-off is almost effortless for most people.

THE BUTTERFLY KICK

This is an excellent way to develop coordination and core muscles. The abdominal kick is called the "butterfly kick" because it emphasizes the abdominal muscles while kicking.

The breaststroke kick is more critical for stroke strength than any other swimming style. The most successful breaststroke swimmers have a unique level of flexibility that allows their legs and feet to hold or grip more water during the kick. Adult swimmers with a history of knee injuries should consider switching to the butterfly stroke in training if they experience pain during the breaststroke.

How many kicks does it take to cover the length of the pool?

Challenge yourself to reduce the number by decreasing the resistance as you pull your heels in, speeding up the propulsion phase, and lengthening the kick.

A mixture of stroke drills swim drills, and complete swim strokes are the ideal way to improve performance.

The release of the stroke is different for distance swimmers and sprint swimmers. Continue the forward swing. If you shrug your shoulders, you can use the inward motion to bring your hands into the prayer position. If you want to improve your timing, swim for less time.

Swimming style varies from swimmer to swimmer, depending on size, strength, and flexibility.

CRAWL DRILLS

The freestyle stroke, commonly referred to as the crawl, is often misunderstood as being powered predominantly by the upper body. However, this is a misconception. The legs play a crucial role in swimming, providing significant propulsion when properly trained and utilized. It is true that the larger muscles of the torso, such as the latissimus dorsi and pectorals, consume more oxygen, but this does not diminish the importance of leg strength and endurance.

To maximize the effectiveness of the crawl, swimmers must develop a balanced and powerful kick. This requires targeted training that focuses on both the downbeat and upbeat of the kick. The downbeat, where the foot moves towards the bottom of the pool, generates the primary propulsive force, while the upbeat, where the foot moves towards the surface, helps to maintain rhythm and contributes to the continuous motion of the legs.

Elite swimmers often maintain a six-beat kick throughout a race, which means they execute six leg kicks per full stroke cycle of the arms. This consistent, high-frequency kicking pattern is essential for maintaining speed and reducing drag. To achieve this, swimmers must possess both the strength and cardiovascular endurance necessary to sustain the kick's intensity over the duration of the race.

Training for the crawl should be approached with the same rigor as strength training. Swimmers should perform high-intensity kicking drills with adequate rest intervals to build power and speed. One effective method is the vertical kick, which can be practiced in deep water using all four competitive strokes. The objective of the vertical kick is to maintain an upright position in the water, with the head and shoulders above the surface, while the legs execute the stroke-specific kick. This drill not only enhances leg strength but also promotes core stability, as the swimmer must engage their abdominal and lower back muscles to remain upright.

The choice of kicking drills should be tailored to the swimmer's individual strengths and experience level. For instance, butterfly stroke performance is heavily reliant on a robust and symmetrical dolphin kick, which utilizes both the upward and downward motions to create lift and propulsion. Breaststroke, on the other hand, requires a different approach, focusing on the core and leg muscles to achieve a smooth gliding motion and an effective whip kick.

Incorporating rowing movements into swimming drills can also be beneficial. These exercises help swimmers understand the relationship between arm positions, the range of motion, and body alignment during the stroke. By practicing various rowing drills, swimmers can improve their catch and pull phases, leading to a more efficient and powerful stroke overall.

The crawl is not merely a test of upper body strength but a full-body effort that demands attention to leg power and technique. By integrating high-intensity kicking drills, vertical kicking, and rowing movements into their training regimen, swimmers can enhance their propulsion and achieve greater speed in the water. With consistent practice, patience, and perseverance, the improvements in leg strength and kicking technique will translate into faster, more efficient swimming.

REFINING THE BUTTERFLY STROKE: EMBRACING FLUIDITY AND CORE ENGAGEMENT

The evolution of the butterfly stroke over the past decade has been marked by a shift towards a flatter, more hydrodynamic approach. Today's elite butterfly swimmers exemplify a model of efficiency, characterized by a rhythmic undulation that originates from the core and extends through the body. This undulation is not merely a stylistic choice but a fundamental aspect of reducing drag and maximizing forward momentum.

The key to mastering this modern butterfly technique lies in the harmonious movement of the torso muscles. These muscles, when engaged correctly, facilitate a wave-like motion that propels the swimmer forward with grace and power. The goal is to achieve a sensation of fluidity, where each movement feels natural and contributes to the overall propulsion.

Drills designed to enhance the butterfly stroke focus on isolating and strengthening the components that drive this fluid motion. One such drill involves maintaining a horizontal position in the water, with the swimmer's arms relaxed at their sides. The head should be aligned with the neck and spine, creating a streamlined profile. As the swimmer executes the undulating motion, the engagement of the abdominal muscles becomes apparent. By pressing the chest slightly downward, the upper abdominals tighten, reinforcing the swimmer's core stability.

Visualizing the legs as an extension of the chest and hips is crucial for transferring energy efficiently. This mental image encourages the swimmer to channel the undulating force from the core through the thighs, knees, shins, and toes. The hips should remain buoyant, riding high on the water's surface, while the feet execute the final propulsive flick. It is essential to maintain a connection between the legs and the core, allowing the strength of the abdominal and hip muscles to dictate the kicking motion.

Minimizing the amplitude of the undulation is another critical aspect of a proficient butterfly stroke. Excessive vertical movement can lead to increased drag and wasted energy. Instead, swimmers should focus on keeping the waves generated by their body as low as possible, emphasizing the forward thrust. This not only conserves energy but also ensures that the swimmer's efforts are directed towards horizontal displacement.

In practice, the butterfly stroke should feel like a cohesive, wave-like motion that seamlessly integrates the upper and lower body. By focusing on core engagement, fluidity, and minimizing vertical displacement, swimmers can refine their butterfly technique to achieve greater efficiency and speed. Through dedicated practice and attention to these details, the butterfly stroke can transform from a physically demanding endeavor into an expression of aquatic finesse.

BUILDING MOMENTUM IS ESSENTIAL

Building momentum in the water is a nuanced process that requires a swimmer to understand and refine the interplay between stroke length, rhythm, and power. To enhance the butterfly stroke, for example, swimmers must focus on the synchronization of their upper and lower body movements. The progression begins with the arms spreading wide to initiate the catch phase, as the chest presses downward. This motion should be fluid and continuous, with the hands pulling back in concert with the undulating movement of the chest and hips. It is crucial to maintain a neutral head position, aligned with the spine, to avoid creating additional drag.

As the swimmer's chest is pressed down during the catch, the hands should accelerate through the water, completing a full pull cycle. This acceleration is not just about moving the hands faster; it is about applying increasing force throughout the underwater phase of the stroke, culminating in a powerful push at the end. Once these elements are mastered—catch, pull, head position, and kick timing—the swimmer can seamlessly transition into the full butterfly stroke.

The forward momentum generated by each stroke should be harnessed to maintain a consistent rhythm, which is essential for efficient swimming over longer distances.
In freestyle sprinting, a robust and rhythmic six-beat kick is

often observed among elite swimmers. These athletes typically possess large, flexible feet and exceptional ankle mobility, which contribute to an effective push-off. However, it is a common misconception that the primary benefit of a strong push-off is to lift the swimmer's body out of the water. In reality, the push-off's main advantage lies in its contribution to forward propulsion, while minimizing the increase in drag that comes with higher speeds.

Sprinters must be cautious not to overemphasize the push-off to the point where it disrupts their stroke mechanics and increases drag disproportionately to the propulsion gained. An overly forceful push-off can lead to a loss of coordination and control, resulting in inefficient energy expenditure. Instead, sprinters should aim for a balanced push-off that complements their natural swimming rhythm, allowing for a smooth transition into the stroke cycle without unnecessary energy waste.

Swimming, being a full-body sport, demands a harmonious activation of the legs, core, and upper body muscles throughout the stroke cycle. Strength training and conditioning are vital components of a swimmer's preparation, as they provide the stability and power needed for peak performance. By developing strength and endurance, swimmers can improve their coordination and maintain proper technique, even as fatigue sets in during a race. This holistic approach to training ensures that swimmers are equipped to draw upon the appropriate energy systems, whether sprinting a short distance or pacing themselves through a longer event.

THE STARTING POINT FOR FORWARD MOVEMENT

The initiation of forward movement in swimming, particularly when starting a race or pushing off from the wall, is a critical skill that can set the tone for the entire swim. To optimize your starts, it is essential to practice in a controlled aquatic environment, where you can focus on technique without the interference of waves or currents.

When preparing for a start, whether from the pool deck or the starting blocks, the alignment of your body is paramount. Begin by standing tall, ensuring your spine is straight. This can be achieved by gently retracting your chin, creating space between your chin and chest, which aligns your head with your spine. Engage your core muscles by tightening your abdomen, and activate your glutes to create a solid base of support. Your feet should be positioned together, toes curled over the edge of the pool or starting block, ready to propel you forward.

As you practice jumping into the water, it is crucial to maintain a streamlined posture. This means extending your arms above your head, hands overlapping with one palm over the back of the other hand, and biceps pressed against your ears. Your body should form a straight line from the tips of your fingers down to your pointed toes. This streamlined shape reduces drag and allows for a more efficient entry into the water.

Resist the natural instinct to lift your head as you dive. Looking up as you enter the water creates unnecessary frontal resistance, which can slow you down and disrupt the fluidity of your movement. Instead, keep your head down, in line with your arms, and focus on piercing the water with the crown of your head, followed by the rest of your body, entering through the same point to minimize splash and resistance.

When using starting blocks, position your feet shoulder-width apart for stability. Your toes should grip the edge of the block, and your body should be coiled with potential energy. The start is not just a jump—it's a powerful drive that engages your hip and leg muscles. As you push off, extend through your hips, knees, and ankles, channeling the force through your legs and off the blocks. Your arms should swing forward in a controlled motion to assist in propelling your body out and over the water.

Remember, the goal is to carry momentum from the blocks into the water, transitioning smoothly into your stroke without losing speed. With consistent practice, your starts will become more explosive and efficient, setting you up for a successful swim.

If you want to increase your strength

To enhance your strength and power off the blocks, it's essential to understand the mechanics of a successful start. Here's how to refine your technique:

Arm Swing: The arm swing is a preparatory motion that helps generate momentum. To perform an effective arm swing, start with your arms relaxed and hanging by your sides. As you prepare to launch off the blocks, swing your arms backward and then swiftly forward and up, extending them above your head in a streamlined position. This motion should be fluid and contribute to the explosive power of your start.

Visualization: Imagine a hula hoop lying flat on the surface of the water directly in front of the starting block. This visualization technique helps you focus on the point of entry. Your goal is to enter the water at the center of this imaginary hoop with minimal splash and maximum forward drive.

Entry: As you swing your arms forward, envision pressing the center of the hula hoop with your fingertips, leading the entry. Your arms should create a circular motion, similar to the path they would take if you were actually trying to move through the hoop. This helps in achieving a clean, sharp entry into the water.

Body Tension: As you drive through the center of the imaginary hoop, it's crucial to keep your body tense and streamlined. A tight core and extended body line will reduce drag and allow you to penetrate the water more effectively, preserving the momentum you've built.

Maintain your streamlined position underwater until you break the surface and transition into your stroke. This underwater phase is where you build momentum, and a seamless transition can set the pace for the rest of your swim.

Regarding the starting technique, the "lane start" is often compared to the "grab start" used in track meets. The lane start is a straightforward approach where swimmers place their feet at the front of the block, grab the block with their hands, and push off at the command. This method is particularly suitable for swimmers with limited mobility or those new to competitive swimming.

For the grab start, position yourself on the block with your feet shoulder-width apart, toes curled over the edge, and your gaze directed down. Avoid resting your chest on your thighs, and keep your head in a neutral position, aligned with your spine. Depending on your flexibility and comfort, you may adjust your foot placement—swimmers with limited mobility may benefit from placing their back foot slightly further back on the block and lowering their hips for a better grip.

When learning the forward start, pull one foot back slightly, bend at the hips, and hold this "set" position for a couple of seconds to establish balance and focus. When the start signal is given, drive off the block with your legs, allowing your body to unfold into a streamlined position above the water as you dive in.

Remember, the key to a powerful start is the combination of a strong, dynamic takeoff, a streamlined entry, and an effective underwater phase. With practice and attention to these details, you can maximize your starting strength and set yourself up for a successful swim.

EXERCISES FOR FORWARD LAUNCHING

To refine your forward launching technique, it's essential to practice exercises that simulate the explosive start required in competitive swimming. One such exercise involves the use of a clap as an auditory cue to initiate a streamlined position. Here's how to perform the exercise effectively:

Starting Position: Begin by assuming your starting position on the block. Your front foot should be at the edge of the block, with your back foot placed comfortably behind, ready to push off. Your body should be coiled with potential energy, much like a spring.

Streamlined Arms: Upon hearing the clap, immediately snap your hands and arms into a streamlined position above your head. Your arms should be straight, with one hand over the other, and biceps pressed against your ears. This position reduces drag and prepares you for a sleek entry into the water.

Back Foot Lift: Simultaneously with the arm movement, lift your back foot off the block to initiate the forward momentum. Your body should uncoil as you drive forward with your legs.

Bar Adjustment Exercise: To practice entering the water cleanly, use an adjustable bar placed over the pool. Start with the bar at a height that requires you to clear it without touching. As you improve, lower the bar to challenge your ability to maintain a tight, streamlined position while clearing it. The goal is to pass over the bar without breaking your form, simulating a clean entry into the water.

THE RELAY BEGINS

In relay races, the exchange between swimmers is a critical component that can significantly impact the outcome of the race. The timing of the relay start is a delicate balance between speed and precision. Here's what each swimmer must do to execute a successful relay start:

Incoming Swimmer: The swimmer in the water must maintain a strong stroke rate and rhythm as they approach the wall. It's crucial to finish with a powerful touch to give their teammate the best chance for a quick start.

Starting Swimmer: The swimmer on the block must watch the incoming swimmer closely. As the incoming swimmer reaches for the wall, the starting swimmer must time their launch so that their feet leave the block the moment the incoming swimmer's hand makes contact with the wall.

This requires anticipation and precise timing to minimize changeover time without incurring a false start.

Forward and Backward Start: In a relay, the first swimmer will typically perform a forward start, using the techniques described earlier to maximize their launch off the block. The last swimmer, however, may need to adjust their start based on the incoming swimmer's finish. If the incoming swimmer is finishing with a backstroke, the starting swimmer must be prepared to execute a backward start, pushing off the wall with their back facing the pool.

By practicing these techniques and understanding the nuances of relay starts, swimmers can shave precious seconds off their relay times, contributing to the overall success of their team.

CONCLUSION

Embarking on the journey to enhance your swimming capabilities is a commitment to self-improvement that pays dividends in speed, endurance, and the sheer joy of gliding through the water. This book serves as a comprehensive guide to help you embark on that journey with confidence and knowledge.

The cornerstone of any successful endeavor in the pool is consistent practice. It's through repetition that the body learns the nuances of each stroke, the mind memorizes the rhythm of breathing, and the spirit becomes resilient to the challenges of training. Improvement in swimming is not instantaneous; it is the result of dedication and the accumulation of hours spent refining your technique.

A robust foundation in swimming is constructed from well-designed exercises that target specific aspects of your performance. These exercises are the building blocks of your training regimen, each one designed to address different components of swimming, from stroke efficiency to power and speed. Neglecting this crucial step in your training is akin to building a house without a blueprint—it may stand temporarily, but it will not withstand the tests of time and competition.

Remember, the path to swimming excellence is a marathon, not a sprint. It requires patience, perseverance, and a willingness to embrace the process of gradual improvement. Each session in the pool is an opportunity to lay another "brick" in your foundation, bringing you one stroke closer to your goals.

As you close this book and prepare for your next swim, carry with you the knowledge that every champion once stood where you are now. They, too, faced the vast expanse of the pool with determination and a vision of what they could achieve. Your journey is unique, and while the road to success is rarely straight, it is the twists and turns that make the story worth telling.

So, dive in with enthusiasm, train with purpose, and never lose sight of the joy that swimming brings. Until we meet again, may your strokes be strong, your breaths be rhythmic, and your passion for the water be unending. Here's to your swimming success—may you find your own "Gold Medal Moment" in the lanes ahead.

This guide is not intended as and may not be construed as an alternative to or a substitute for professional mental counseling, therapy, legal or medical services and advice.

The authors, publishers, and distributors of this guide have made every effort to ensure the validity, accuracy, and timely nature of the information presented here. However, no guarantee is made, neither direct nor implied, that the information in this guide or the techniques described herein are suitable for or applicable to any given individual person or group of persons, nor that any specific result will be achieved. The authors, publishers, and distributors of this guide will be held harmless and without fault in all situations and causes arising from the use of this information by any person, with or without professional supervision. The information contained in this book is for informational and entertainment purposes only. It's not intended as a professional advice or a recommendation to act.

No part of this book may be reproduced or transmitted in any form whatsoever, electronic, or mechanical, including photocopying, recording, or by any informational storage or retrieval system without express permission from the author.

Click here to get it

https://know.howtobeon.top/healthy

© Copyright 2022, Zee Publishing
Date of publication June 2022
All rights reserved.